Curios
of
Leicestershire
and Rutland

A County Guide
to the Unusual
by
Joyce Lee and Jon Dean

S.B. Publications

CONTENTS

RUTLAND

Front Cover: Worthington Lock-up.
Back Cover: Clipsham Yew Tree Avenue.
Title Page: The Seagrave Serpent and Ophicleide.

ACKNOWLEDGEMENTS

Mrs. A.L. Atton (Leicestershire Constabulary); Lt. Col. E.H.L. Aubrey-Fletcher (Stanford Hall); Mrs. Briggs (Kibworth Harcourt); Wing Commander J.H. Smith-Carington (Ashby Folville); Claybrooke Mill; Terry Coltman (Loughborough Carillon); Martie Cowley (Lubenham); Mary Handley (Osgathorpe); W.D. Maltby (Worthington Parish Council); D.R. Minkley (Burton-on-the-Wolds); Staff of Rothley Court Hotel and Bosworth Hall Hotel; Mrs. H. Steele (Breedon-on-the-Hill); A.V. Sadler; Stoney Cove Marine Trials Ltd; John Taylor & Co. (Bellfounders) Ltd; Wardens of Ravenstone Hospital; Jeremy Winter (Coleorton Hall).

Staff at the Leicestershire Record Office especially Aubrey Stevenson and Mike Raftery; Staff of Leicestershire County Council's Planning and Transportation Department's Historic Buildings section; Museum curators and volunteers especially at Wigston Framework Knitters Museum, Moira Blast Furnace and Oakham Castle.

David Potter (Hinckley Times) and Phillip Lindley (Hinckley Library) for the story of Hinckley's Tin Hat.

Incumbents, officials, volunteers and keyholders of Leicestershire and Rutland churches; farmers; park wardens; and the many other people who helped provide information, directions and help.

Leicestershire Museums, Arts and Records Service for permission to publish the photograph of the horseshoes at Oakham Castle.

THE AUTHORS

JOYCE LEE

Brought up in Coventry, Joyce Lee has lived and worked in Leicestershire for over twenty years. She has written and lectured on local studies topics and is the author of *Who's buried where in Leicestershire*. She studied at both Leicester and Loughborough Universities and has degrees in archaeology, history and librarianship. After leaving university she worked for Leicester's Tourist Information Office and then for Leicestershire Libraries and Information Service where for a number of years she worked closely with the Local Studies Collection. She is currently systems manager for Leicestershire Libraries main computer system. Her interests include exploring Leicestershire and Rutland, history, walking and travel.

JON DEAN

Jon Dean is from Leicester. He studied mathematics and sociology at Cambridge and Leicester Universities, graduating in 1975. This was followed by a varied career in local government ranging from housing to engineering and information technology. He currently works as a systems analyst for Leicestershire County Council. His interests include railways, gardening, bridge, music, general knowledge quizzes, local history and walking.

INTRODUCTION

Leicestershire and Rutland are amongst the less well-known parts of the country. Situated in the heart of the shire counties, they form an area "off the beaten track", of unexpected variety, with much to offer and many hidden gems and delights to discover. The landscape ranges from the rolling hills and rural tranquillity of Rutland and east Leicestershire; and the beautiful villages of the Vale of Belvoir in the north east; to the more rugged countryside of Charnwood and the north west; and the pleasant farm and pasture land of the south. In the centre is Leicester, a city of contrasts and surprises, and scattered around the county are a number of attractive market towns.

Along the roadsides, in the villages, towns, churches and buildings of this area, are a fascinating variety of curious and unusual features. It is the aim of this book to provide an illustrated guide to almost a hundred such "curiosities", to explain their purpose, and to provide some indication of their history.

Spanning the centuries from Saxon times right up to the present day, these include a unique collection of ceremonial horseshoes; a rare finger pillory; the oldest stained glass window in England, and a mysterious turf maze. Among survivals of a bygone age are once common features of village life such as lock-ups, stocks, windmills, crosses, wells and pumps. There are also eccentric tombs; unusual epitaphs and notable monuments; buildings with strange tales attached; objects with unusual connections; follies; feats of engineering; and unexpected legacies of the industrial age.

There are many more curiosities in Leicestershire and Rutland in addition to those described here, and it is hoped that this book will not only stimulate further interest and research, but also encourage the preservation of this unique aspect of the past.

The majority of the sites listed are readily accessible. A few however are situated on private land and require permission from the owner to visit. Where sites have restricted opening times, it is strongly recommended to enquire locally for details before making a special journey.

Finally, it is the authors' hope that this book will provide a useful and enjoyable guide to some of the many fascinating, unusual and eccentric features of Leicestershire and Rutland, and show that there's much more to the area than pork pies, hunting and Stilton cheese!

Joyce Lee and Jon Dean

ASHBY-DE-LA-ZOUCH
FINGER PILLORY

Location: Inside St. Helen's Church. SK360168

Perpetrators of unruly behaviour in church may once have found themselves doing public penance with their fingers trapped in this device. Known as a finger pillory, the principle was similar to the stocks, the difference being that it held fingers rather than ankles. It consists of a horizontal wooden jaw-like arm about three feet long which opens up to reveal thirteen holes of various sizes. The lower part of the arm is fixed and is supported by the church wall at one end and an upright post at the other. The upper section is hinged at the wall end. It worked by one of the offender's fingers being placed in a hole of the appropriate size. The hinged top was then brought down and clamped by a lock at the other end, making it impossible to withdraw the finger. This left the finger in a most uncomfortable crooked position.

Very few finger pillories still exist, this one at Ashby being a rare survival. Thought to date from the seventeenth century, it is uncertain how long it was used for, but contemporary accounts show that it had passed into history by the end of the eighteenth century.

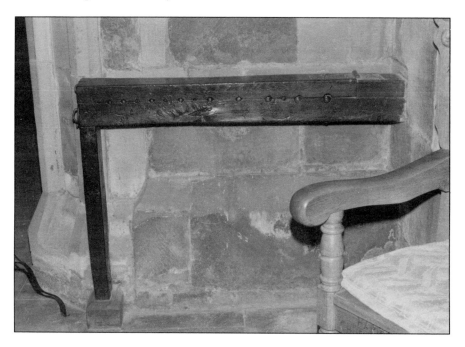

BELTON
A PERMANENT MAYPOLE

Location: Village centre, opposite the George Hotel.   SK447208

Belton has the distinction of having one of the few permanent maypoles left in the country, with the village boasting a tradition of maypole dancing going back at least 200 years. The pole is painted in the customary red, white and blue, with a globe and running fox weather-vane on the top. It is the latest in a series of poles to have stood in the centre of Belton, and is relatively short compared with some of its predecessors, one of which is recorded as being a staggering twenty-six yards high.

Over the years, Belton's maypole has had a chequered history, providing a focal point for inter-village rivalry between Belton and neighbouring Shepshed on more then one occasion. Local tradition tells how around the turn of the twentieth century a gang from Shepshed stole the pole after having been beaten by Belton at football. Later, during the World War II blackout, the pole was knocked down by a reversing bus. A new pole was subsequently put up in the early 1950s. More recently on Boxing Night in 1983 the pole was sawn off and left "planted" in a Shepshed park. It has since been re-erected. Today, Belton continues to keep the tradition of May Day celebrations alive in an annual event which attracts a wide audience.

BRADGATE PARK
OLD JOHN TOWER

Location: Near Newtown Linford, approached from several paths in the park. SK526112

Old John is Leicestershire's best-known folly, prominently situated close to the highest point in Bradgate Park. The park is an area of outstanding beauty, containing some of the oldest rocks in England and at its centre are the ruins of Lady Jane Grey's childhood home.

According to tradition, the tower commemorates a local miller known as "Old John", who in 1786, along with many others, was at the park celebrating the coming-of-age of the Earl of Stamford's eldest son. A huge bonfire had been lit, in the middle of which was a large pole surrounded by faggots and tar barrels. As the fire burned, the pole burnt through at the bottom, and suddenly fell into the crowd, killing Old John on the spot. On hearing the news, the Earl, for whom Old John was a particular favourite, decreed that a tower should be erected to his memory, its distinctive beer mug shape a reminder of the miller's fondness for ale. Built on the spot where his windmill had stood, the tower became known as "Old John". Recent research has, however, cast doubts on this story, suggesting that it was more likely built as a hunting tower in 1784. Similar in design to the folly on top of Mow Cop in Cheshire, it is thought that John Hope, a Cheshire architect, was responsible for both structures.

BRADGATE PARK
POLICE BOX

Location:	Newtown Linford entrance to Bradgate Park. SK523097

This pale blue box just inside the gates at the Newtown Linford entrance to Bradgate Park is exceptional in that it is thought to be the last working police box in Britain. It is still used both by special constables patrolling the park during summer weekends, and at other times by regular police patrols. Approximately six feet square, the box contains a telephone, first-aid kit, desk and log book.

Boxes like this were an innovation of the 1930s and played an important part in the policing of rural areas. They radically improved communications, enabling officers to be contacted more quickly, and reduced the length of time taken to get to incidents.

The first boxes in Leicestershire were at Lutterworth, Arnesby, North Kilworth and Ullesthorpe, followed shortly afterwards by Buckminster, Twyford and Scalford. The designer was the county architect William Keay. However, by the late 1960s, the boxes were no longer needed and were taken out of service with the exception of the box at Bradgate. Originally from North Kilworth, it was moved to the park in 1952 and fortunately is now destined to be preserved.

BREEDON-ON-THE-HILL
LOCK-UP AND PINFOLD

> *Location:* Main Street, opposite The Three Horse Shoes. Beware of traffic.
> SK406228

Here at Breedon is Leicestershire's best-known surviving example of a village roundhouse or lock-up. These primitive buildings largely date from the eighteenth century and were the forerunners of police cells. They were used to hold suspects awaiting trial, and more frequently as an overnight village "cooler" for drunkards and disturbers of the peace (q.v. Worthington).

As can be seen at Breedon, a night spent locked up here would have been extremely unpleasant. Referred to locally as the "dark hole", the only light and ventilation comes in through a small grille in the heavy solid door. Built entirely of stone, the thick walls would have muffled any noise made by the miscreants.

Fragments of Breedon's former priory can be spotted incorporated into the outside wall, whilst adjoining the lock-up is the village pinfold.

BREEDON-ON-THE-HILL
SAXON CARVINGS

Location: Inside St. Mary and St. Hardulph Church. SK405233

Breedon church forms an impressive landmark for miles around. It stands high on the hill above the village, with a sheer drop on one side down to the quarry below. The church is renowned for its Saxon sculpture, unequalled anywhere else in the country. This outstanding series of carvings includes over seventy feet of frieze and panels. Most of these are now embedded within the walls inside the church.

Dating from the eighth century, there are four groups to look out for. These include a narrow frieze of interlaced vine scrolls; a deeper frieze with animals,

birds and human figures; a series of figure panels set in arches, and fourthly the remains of decorated cross fragments. The most famous of the carvings is in the tower. This is the Breedon Angel, said to be the earliest known carved angel in the country. All the friezes are cut in high relief. The source of inspiration for the carvings is thought to have been contemporary illuminated manuscripts produced at the monastery which formerly stood on the site. Both the church itself and the Saxon carvings are depicted on an attractive stained glass window behind the altar. Most of the carvings can be viewed whenever the church is open but to see the Breedon Angel requires access by key to the tower ringing chamber.

CASTLE DONINGTON
KEY HOUSE

Location: 20 High Street.   SK443271

Access: Privately owned. View from the roadside.

Castle Donington is probably the best-preserved small town in Leicestershire. Among its many interesting older buildings is Key House, an attractive black-and-white timber-framed house which certainly lives up to its name. Hanging high up on different gables facing the road are three of its keys. Two are actual metal keys, the third painted on, each with a date by it. Two of them also have initials by them. "T.R." is for Thomas Robey who built the house in 1636. Since then the house has been extended and altered over the years. Don't be misled by the earlier date of 1595 by the key on the distinctive overhanging two storied porch, as this part of the building was actually removed to here from an older house opposite. By the third key is the date 1899 and initials H.R.T., whilst in more recent years another much larger key has been added on the side of the building with the dates 1953–81 and the initials F.W.M.

Key House features strongly in Castle Donington folklore: one story tells how an old woman who once lived there had a son who went to be a sailor. She hung the key outside so that he could get in without trouble should he ever come home. Another tale tells of a jealous husband who locked up his wild young wife in the house and hung up the key outside to prevent her escaping!

COLEORTON
WORDSWORTH MEMORIALS

Location: Coleorton Hall Grounds.   SK392174

Access: Strictly by prior arrangement only.

It has been claimed that Coleorton Hall grounds possess more memorials to the poet William Wordsworth than anywhere else in England, including Rydal Mount. This extraordinary collection is the result of Wordsworth's friendship with Sir George Howland Beaumont (1753–1827), who built the present hall and was a great patron of the arts.

In October 1806, Wordsworth came to stay at nearby Hall Farm as a guest of Sir George and lived there with his family until the following June. Further visits followed in 1810 and during the 1820s and a number of Wordsworth's poems were inspired by his stays at Coleorton. Visible remains of Wordsworth's connections include the hall's Winter Garden which he designed whilst living at Hall Farm, and the stone memorials in the hall's grounds which are engraved with his verses. These include the tribute on the cenotaph to artist Sir Joshua Reynolds, and a memorial honouring the Elizabethan dramatist Sir Francis Beaumont, which includes Wordsworth's description of the local Charnwood hills. It was rumoured that the head gardener allowed Wordsworth to undertake the winter garden to keep him occupied and out of his way! It is this part of the garden which has the rock seat created by Wordsworth where Sir Walter Scott is said to have sat whilst writing his novel "Ivanhoe".

COSSINGTON
AN EARLY CHURCH CLOCK

Location: All Saints Church. SK603137

Saxon sundials, scratch and mass dials were early forms of church clocks which preceded the more elaborate sundials and mechanical clocks. They look like geometric drawings and are often quite hard to spot. The earliest examples date back to Anglo-Saxon times, the later ones are medieval. They were used to indicate the times of prayers, services, and when to ring the bell for the canonical hours, and are normally to be found on an external south-facing church wall, usually at eye level. One of the best-preserved examples in Leicestershire can be seen here at All Saints Church, Cossington. It is carefully carved with ten equal radial lines inside a double half circle with well-proportioned Roman numerals around the edge. Although the earliest surviving church fabric is Norman, the dial bears a greater resemblance to a Saxon sundial than to the later more crudely "scratched" or mass dials. There is an obvious hole in the middle where a peg would have been, casting a shadow which would have indicated the time from sunrise to sunset.

Also of interest in Cossington churchyard is the external vestry room erected in 1835 and once used by Thomas Cook for his early Temperance group tour meetings, whilst outside the east window is the grave of Lord Kitchener's father.

GARENDON
AN EIGHTEENTH-CENTURY LANDSCAPE

Location: Near M1 Junction 23, north of A512, on private land. SK498190

Access: View from a distance from the roadside. No public access.

On the outskirts of Loughborough are the unexpected remains of an eighteenth-century classical landscape. The intriguing green dome in the middle of a field near to the M1 motorway, and the tall obelisk about a mile away on the edge of the Thorpe Acre housing estate both belong to the Garendon Park estate, and are reminders of one of Leicestershire's vanished great houses. They were the work of Ambrose Phillipps, a "gentleman architect" with a keenness for classical architecture who inherited the estate in 1729. Phillipps also wrote poetry and has the distinction of being the person for whom the phrase "namby-pamby" was first coined on account of his sentimental verse.

Garendon's green dome is part of the Temple of Venus, modelled by Phillipps on the Temple of Vesta in Rome. A statue of Venus once stood inside but was destroyed in 1811, possibly by Luddite rioters. Not far away, but almost out of view, is a further structure, the Triumphal Arch, based on the Arch of Titus, also in Rome. At one time, rooms on either side of the archway served as accommodation for the estate's gamekeeper. Garendon House itself was rebuilt by Phillipps' descendants, but was eventually demolished after a fire in 1964. As part of this inglorious end, some 3,500 tons of hardcore from the building were used in the construction of the nearby M1 Motorway.

GLENFIELD
HISTORIC RAILWAY TUNNEL

Location: Approach by footpath off A50 near Faire Road (involves some fifty steps) or from Loxley Road in Glenfield. SK544065

The Leicester and Swannington Railway was one of the earliest steam railway lines in the world. Opened in July 1832, the line was primarily constructed to carry coal from north-west Leicestershire to Leicester. Amongst the railway's more substantial remains is this tunnel entrance by Robert Stephenson, now hidden behind a housing estate. Stephenson's plans for an elaborate portal of Mountsorrel granite were never carried out due to the expense and the original brickwork was retained. At 1,796 yards, Glenfield tunnel was for a while the longest in England. It was also has the distinction of being the second railway tunnel in the world to be used for passenger traffic.

Originally there were large gates at both entrances of the tunnel which were closed at night to keep out curious local people. A variety of primitive methods were used to prevent trains from colliding on the single track inside. These included flags, candles, and at one time fifteen-minute sand-glasses at either end of the tunnel. The line closed to passenger traffic in 1928 and completely in 1966. The Leicester entrance to the tunnel has since been filled in, but the tops of several of the ventilation shafts can still be seen, at least one of which is in a front garden. Suggestions for reusing the tunnel have ranged from growing mushrooms to a night-club, but none have come to fruition.

LOUGHBOROUGH
A CARILLON FOR A WAR MEMORIAL

Location: Queen's Park, town centre.   SK533193

The distinctive green-topped tower which dominates Loughborough's skyline is a unique War Memorial. When suggestions were invited for a monument to the town's fallen in World War I, local builder Mr. Wilfred Moss came forward with the unusual idea of a tower and bell carillon along the lines of those common in Flanders where so many had lost their lives. The proposal was agreed and public subscriptions were invited to meet the costs. Local bell founders Taylors (q.v.) were commissioned to cast the bells and Walter Tapper was chosen as architect. The inspiration for the design came from the medieval belfry at Moulins in

France. Erected during 1922–3 at a cost of £22,000, the Loughborough Carillon was officially opened in July 1923 and was the first carillon war memorial and the first grand carillon in Great Britain.

The carillon consists of forty-seven bells housed in a chamber near the top of the tower. The bells are hung in order of size in a steel frame with the largest at the bottom. Every bell is dedicated, the majority to those who did not return, some in grateful thanks to those who did. The bells are played from a clavier in the room immediately below, by striking the "keyboard" with the fists, a job requiring considerable skill and stamina on the part of the carilloneur. The tower and its museum are open during the summer when regular recitals are also given.

LOUGHBOROUGH
A WORLD FAMOUS BELL FOUNDRY

Location: John Taylor & Co.(Bellfounders) Ltd. Freehold Street. SK540194

With some justification Loughborough could be called the town of the bells. Not only is it the home of the famous Carillon (q.v.), but also home to Taylors Bell Foundry, one of the few places in the country where bells are still made, and said to be the largest bell-foundry complex in the world.

The company have been casting and recasting bells since 1784. The works at Loughborough were set up by John Taylor in the middle of the nineteenth century and since then the firm has gained a worldwide reputation. Famous individual bells cast by Taylors include "Great Paul" of St. Paul's Cathedral, London. This was despatched by road from the Loughborough works in May 1882, the spectacular procession travelling via Leicester, Oadby and Kibworth. Almost two weeks later it arrived in London. Weighing in at 37,483 lbs, this is the largest and heaviest bell ever hung in Great Britain. Complete rings of bells and carillons made by Taylors can be found throughout the world from Australia to South Africa and America, as well as throughout Britain. The processes involved in bellfounding can be seen by appointment on guided tours of the works. There is also a bell-foundry museum which is regularly open to the public.

LOUGHBOROUGH

A COMMEMORATIVE WEATHER-VANE

Location: Hazlerigg Hall, Loughborough University.   SK521192

Leicestershire has a number of eccentric weather-vanes on both private and public buildings, but perhaps one of the most individual is this one at Loughborough University. A unique memorial, it depicts the silhouetted figure of Dr. Herbert Schofield, who as principal of Loughborough College from 1915–50, built it up to be an outstanding educational institution on which the subsequent reputation of Loughborough University was established. A flamboyant character, energetic entrepreneur and outstanding educationalist, Dr. Schofield was held in high regard by both his students and staff. The episode illustrated on the weather vane refers to the frequent transatlantic trips he made to America both for business and to attend international Rotary meetings. Designed by Captain E.G. Fowler, the architect to the County Education Committee, the weather-vane was the finishing touch to the College's Hazlerigg Hall of Residence when it opened in June 1938. It features Dr. Schofield's running figure, case in hand and wearing one of his characteristic wide-brimmed American hats, hurrying towards a liner. At the opposite end is a group of students, one on his knees, those in the middle waving a sad goodbye, whilst another at the back cries into a handkerchief. By the 1960s the weather-vane had become badly worn but fortunately staff from the university saw to it that the original was replaced by an exact replica.

14

MOIRA
BLAST FURNACE

Location: Furnace Lane. SK314152

Access: Grounds open all year. Enquire locally for opening times of the Furnace Museum.

This prominent and strange-looking building is said to be one of the best-preserved blast furnaces in Europe. The main reason for its remarkable condition is that it had an exceptionally short working life. Built in 1804, it was part of attempts by local landowner Francis Rawdon Hastings, Second Earl of Moira, to exploit the coal and ironstone from his estates in the area. Iron production commenced in 1806, but less than a year later the furnace was shut down as operating costs were not being covered. Another unsuccessful attempt was made in 1810 and after this no further iron-smelting was undertaken, although the site continued in use as a foundry until the middle of the nineteenth century. The buildings were subsequently turned into unusual living accommodation, some remaining inhabited right up until the early 1970s.

Perhaps the most mysterious features of the furnace are the small arches which are part of the external brickwork. These have attracted much speculation, and may have been intended to help keep the building stable under the high temperatures required inside for making the iron. In the adjacent building which used to be the bridge house is a fascinating museum which includes a model reconstruction of the site. Opposite the museum are the foundations of the engine house, where a large steam-powered beam engine once provided the air blast for the furnace.

OSGATHORPE

A FIVE-SIDED SUNDIAL

Location: St. Mary's Churchyard.   SK431196

One of Leicestershire's most unusual and puzzling sundials can be found by the entrance of Osgathorpe churchyard. It consists of a square block of weathered stone mounted on a more recent short round concrete pillar. No less than five sides of the block each have a sundial and gnomon. The remains of carved lines and numbers for the hours can be seen on some of the faces.

Similar sundial heads exist elsewhere in Britain, some on the top of signposts, others on old stone crosses. In some instances these were part of deliberate attempts to reuse and dignify earlier crosses which had been systematically damaged as part of the anti-Popery campaigns during Elizabethan times and the Commonwealth. Other sundial heads served more decorative purposes. At present it is not known where the Osgathorpe head came from but it is likely that it once topped an ancient cross somewhere, as yet unknown.

RAVENSTONE
ALMSHOUSES

Location: Corner of Hospital Lane and Main Street. SK401139

Situated on the edge of the north-west Leicestershire coalfield, Ravenstone is one of the prettiest and most interesting villages in the area. Amongst its charms is Ravenstone Hospital, a remarkable group of almhouses, notable in a village setting for their sheer monumental scale.

Founded in 1711 to provide accommodation for thirty poor women, the homes were the gift of John and Rebecca Wilkins in memory of their son Francis. For many years the main entrance was from the Ashby Road, and it is on this side where the original foundation plaque can be found. The dwellings were built around a quadrangle and are unusual in that all their entrances face outwards. Notice also the curious lack of guttering at the eaves. Within the central courtyard is an old communal wash-house. In 1784, two identical detached wings with semi-circular ends were added, one for a chapel, the other as the chaplain's house. Although the latter has been sold in recent years, the chapel still serves its original purpose. From the outside it looks like a domestic building — it even has convincing false moulded windows facing the road, with "trompe d'oeil" painted frames and glass. Four further dwellings were added in a separate building in 1860. Today the Hospital is home to twenty-five residents and the courtyard chapel may be visited by enquiring at the Warden's flat.

ROTHLEY
ANTI-SLAVERY MEMORIAL

> *Location:*   On the lawn in front of Rothley Court Hotel. SK577123

This stone pillar in the grounds of Rothley Court Hotel commemorates the historic site where the great philanthropist and reformer William Wilberforce is said to have drafted the parliamentary bill which was to lead to the abolition of slavery in the British Empire. At the time, Wilberforce had been staying at the house as a guest of the Babington family who then lived there. He was a close friend of the family, particularly of Thomas Babington, who was five times MP for Leicester and himself an ardent advocate of the anti-slavery cause.

The memorial was erected a century and a half later by T. Clive Wormleighton in December 1959 when the house was converted to an hotel. It also commemorates the centenary of the death of the famous historian Lord Macaulay who was born here in 1800.

Rothley Court has a long and fascinating history. Originally it belonged to the Knights Templars whose thirteenth-century chapel in the grounds is regarded as the best surviving Templars chapel in the country after the Temple in London.

SWANNINGTON
INCLINED PLANE

Location: Between Coalville and Swannington, signed from Spring Lane. SK418160

The Swannington Incline is a remarkable survival of one of the world's earliest railway lines (q.v. Glenfield Tunnel). Too steep for normal steam locomotives, this end section of the Leicester and Swannington Railway line was worked by a stationary steam engine. The power from this was used to haul up wagons full of coal from the nearby collieries from the bottom to the top of the incline by means of a rope-and-pulley system. At the top the wagons were taken away by train to Leicester.

The rails and pulley system have gone, but the full half-mile length of the incline along the one-in-seventeen gradient can be walked. Information boards along the way describe the site. Starting from the top, the route passes the foundations of the old engine house. There are plans to restore this building and also to bring back the stationary engine from the National Railway Museum at York. Lower down is a restored footbridge taking the ancient green road known as Potato Lane over the incline. The original abutments can still be seen. The next bridge is a recent replacement for Robert Stephenson's original stone one. The third and last bridge has attractive railings made by local craftsmen in 1986. Near here is the foot of the incline, and beyond this point the lines branched off to the various collieries.

SWITHLAND
A DOG LOVER'S ECCENTRIC TOMB

Location: St. Leonard's Churchyard. SK555128

Family pets have long been accorded their own gravestones and sometimes elaborate memorials, but here at Swithland, tradition has it that local squire Sir Joseph Danvers (1686–1753) went one step further. Unwilling to be parted in death from his favourite dog, he wanted the animal to be able to share his grave. However, the parson would not agree. In the end, a compromise was reached, resulting in one of the most unusual and eccentric graves in Leicestershire. The land next to the churchyard belonged to Danvers' own estate — consequently he had his tomb built into the churchyard wall, part of it inside the churchyard, part extended outside onto his own land, so that he could be buried on the consecrated side, with his dog in the adjoining unconsecrated ground. His tomb is also notable for its exquisite slate carvings, amongst the finest in the county. On one side are scenes of ploughing and building, on the other a foreign castle, a ship at sea and a church and hills in the background. The craftsman was John Hind.

Also in the village are two curious round towers set in the corners of a roadside wall. These are locally said to have been lock-ups, but are more likely to have been gazebos or follies used as estate boundary markers.

WORTHINGTON
LOCK-UP

Location: Corner of Church Street and St. Matthews Avenue. SK408206

Standing sentinel at the entrance to Worthington's St. Matthews Avenue estate is this tall strange-looking well-preserved octagonal red-brick structure. Built many years before the houses, it dates from the end of the eighteenth century and was one of several similar buildings in the Leicestershire-Derbyshire border area. Its use was simliar to that at Breedon (q.v.) as a place for the local constable to hold suspected criminals and to temporarily detain local rowdies and drunkards, and it remained in

use until the establishment of the Police Force with its own proper police stations in the following century.

The tall pointed roof, the absence of windows and solid door were all designed to prevent suspects from escaping. The small grille on one side is thought to have been inserted during World War II for defence purposes. A pinfold also stood alongside until recently. In 1947 responsibility for the lock-up was passed to the parish council from Lord Ferrers. Today it is maintained by North West Leicestershire District Council.

ASHBY FOLVILLE
CHURCH DOOR HORSESHOES

Location: St. Mary's Church. SK706119

Fixed to an outside door of St. Mary's Church at Ashby Folville are these two strange-looking horseshoes. The larger one, clearly too big for any horse to wear, is sixteen inches long and almost a foot wide, with straight sides and seventeen three-inch-long thin spikes projecting outwards. The smaller one measures seven by six inches, has curved sides and no spikes. The origins and purpose of both are something of a mystery, although elsewhere in the country, horseshoes were traditionally nailed to church doors to deter malicious witches. These examples are close copies of an earlier pair which dated back to at least the eighteenth century. By the 1890s, the originals had been "wantonly destroyed" and a letter appeared in a local history magazine indicating that the writer, Mr. Smith Carington, owner of the Ashby Folville Estate, proposed "replacing the horseshoes with modern ones as near to the form of the originals as can be produced." Certainly those on the church door today are very similar in appearance to those illustrated in Nichols' County History.

The interior of St. Mary's is one of the most beautiful and interesting in Leicestershire. Amongst its unusual treasures are a superbly carved set of medieval musicians; the church's original stone altar top; a seventeenth-century hourglass holder; and a monument carved with a head and feet at both ends.

ASHBY FOLVILLE
THE FOLVILLE CROSS

| *Location:* | One mile north-east of Ashby Folville, on private land near the Pasture Lane crossroads. SK714134 |

This short upright stone is a lasting reminder of a medieval reign of terror by the infamous Folville family. Described as the most lawless gang of bandits that ever dominated the Leicestershire countryside since the Norman Conquest, their catalogue of criminal activities includes murder, kidnapping, robbery, cattle-stealing and intimidation. Their most notorious case surrounds the death of Sir Roger Beler, a judge and baron of the Exchequer, who became involved in a dispute with gang member Sir Eustace Folville over which of them owned a piece of land in the Ashby Folville area. According to one story, a duel took place near Ashby Pastures to settle the matter, but since Sir Roger was an old man, murder seems more likely. Either way, local tradition states that the stone cross at Pasture Lane marks the spot where Sir Roger met his death. A less colourful alternative story is that the stone was erected as a way-marker for pilgrims travelling between Leicestershire and Nottinghamshire.

Sir Eustace himself was killed in a later duel and buried in St. Mary's Church, Ashby Folville (q.v.), where he is commemorated by an effigy of a knight in chain mail. The knight's chest is tellingly pierced by the point of a lance.

BARSBY
GODSON'S FOLLY

Location: Baggrave End. SK699113

Access: Privately owned. View from the roadside.

This particular building was described in the 1930s as one of the most peculiar dwelling houses in England. It looks like a church but it has never been used as one.

It was built some time before World War I, the original construction consisting of one small room with a high tower. The architect of the scheme was the Rev. J. Godson, a former vicar of Ashby Folville. With no church at Barsby, when a death occured in the village, the inhabitants had to carry the coffin to the

neighbouring village of Ashby Folville. Aware of this inconvenience, Godson intended the building to be the village mortuary chapel to obviate this need. However, because the Bishop had not been consulted and his approval had not been sought for the plan in advance, the request to dedicate the building was refused. Consequently Godson was left with an edifice of limited usefulness. It was his successor, the Rev. Hamper who solved the problem, converting it into a house by increasing its length and adding an extra storey. Since then, the building has had a variety of uses, and as a house today continues to bear the name of "Godson's Folly".

BOTTESFORD

WITCHCRAFT, STOCKS AND WHIPPING POST

> *Location:* St. Mary's Church and Market Street. SK807391

St. Mary's Bottesford is one of the largest village churches in England, the chancel full of awe-inspiring monuments to the Earls of Rutland, lords of nearby Belvoir Castle. Amongst these tombs is a chilling reminder of a famous case of witchcraft. The uniquely worded inscription on the ceiling-high seventeenth-century monument to the Sixth Earl tells how his two young sons "Dyed in their infancy by wicked practise and sorcerye". Thought to be the only tomb in England which gives witchcraft as the cause of death, the case involved Joan Flower and her daughters, all servants at the Castle. Enraged by her daughter Margaret's dismissal from service for allegedly pilfering, Joan is said to have taken revenge by causing the unnatural deaths of both the Earl's sons. Charged with witchcraft, Joan and her daughters were taken off to Lincoln gaol. On the way there, she called for bread saying that if she was guilty then it would choke her. It apparently did, thus confirming her guilt to those present.

St. Mary's has the tallest church spire in Leicestershire. It also has the distinction of being the last place to be attacked by enemy aircraft during World War II.

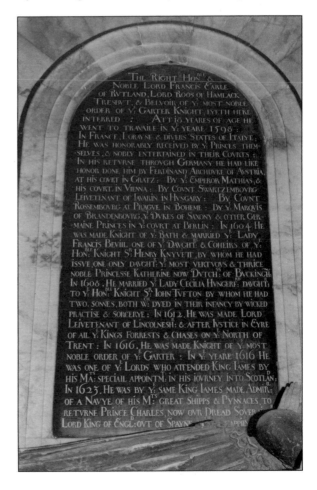

25

In the centre of Bottesford village, the old stocks, whipping post and ancient cross form an interesting group. The cross is over 500 years old and has shields on all four sides of its base, bearing the defaced arms of the de Roos family, the medieval lords of the manor. By the cross are the combined stocks and whipping post. These date from the eighteenth century and have been moved at least once as old photographs show. The whipping post which forms one side of the stocks still has its iron shackles, used to restrain offenders by the wrist. The leg holes of the stocks are now partially below ground level, the surrounding area having been paved over with slates, at least one of which is visibly an old gravestone.

BURTON-ON-THE-WOLDS
LION'S MOUTH FOUNTAIN

Location: Village centre, B676. Beware of traffic. SK589211

Set into the wall of the grounds of Burton Hall is one of Leicestershire's most attractive roadside water features. It is fed from a natural spring which rises in the Hall grounds and is then piped underground. It comes out from the cast-iron lion's mouth set in a stone niche in the wall, into an elliptical stone drinking dish below. There used to be a drinking ladle but this has long since gone. Dating from the middle of the nineteenth century, the fountain is renowned for its reliability even during the most severe droughts. The flow from the spring has rarely stopped: once in recent years when new houses were being built in the grounds of the estate, and once earlier this century when a decomposed mole slowed down the rate of flow for a few days.

Before mains water arrived in Burton, the fountain provided the only source of fresh daily water for those villagers without their own well. It was also a popular stop for horses travelling along the main road through the village.

CROXTON KERRIAL
A ROADSIDE WATER SPOUT

Location: On the A607 near the Peacock Inn. SK833289

Passed by hundreds of motorists daily, it looks like an old petrol pump with liquid endlessly pouring from it. It is, however, one of several roadside water spouts in the area and was built as part of an ingenious local system which captured water from the surrounding hillside springs to provide a water supply to the village. Some of the water collected was fed into a series of ponds near the spout. One of these was known locally as the "Horse Pond", and had a shallow

end where cows and horses were brought to drink. Water from here was also used to fill a smaller brick-built pond which was used to dip sheep prior to shearing. Although part of the system disappeared some time ago when the road was widened, the spout and the pond above it have survived. Water from the spout falls into a drain and flows off down the opposite side of the road towards the River Devon. The supply was still in use in the late 1880s and has never been known to fail apart from when the flow has been accidentally blocked. Croxton was also provided for by water from wells in addition to springs and there is a renovated pump standing close by the church.

EDMONDTHORPE
HERE BE A DRAGON

Location: Main Street. SK862177

Most village pumps are made of cast iron or lead and encased in a modest wooden box. Here at Edmonthorpe is something on an altogether different scale. Outside the old school, now the village social club, is this exceptional outsize pump about eight feet high. Solidly built in the Victorian era, its tapering cast-iron side-panels give it a pyramidal appearance. A monster pump in more ways than one, the spout from which water once flowed is shaped as a dragon's head.

Edmondthorpe owes this unusual village feature to former estate owner William Ann Pochin whose initials appear on the pump, and who also helped to restore the village church and school. On both the pump and the former school building is the Pochin family crest — a winged body with a woman's face.

29

GRIMSTON
STOCKS

Location: The Green. SK683218

Stocks were once a commonplace sight. They have a long history dating back to the Middle Ages when every town and village was obliged to provide their own. Today a few sets have been carefully preserved, of which four survive in Leicestershire and Rutland (q.v. Market Overton, Bottesford and Oakham.) Those at Grimston are typical with two pairs of ankle-holes and upright posts at each end. They stand on the village green in a picturesque, tranquil setting beneath the large chestnut tree planted to commemorate the diamond jubilee of Queen Victoria.

Immediately behind the stocks is a large irregular standing stone. Some sources say it is of historic significance, although according to another it was rolled into the village within living memory. The aptly named "Olde Stocks Restaurant" faces the green. A short walk away is Grimston Church, well worth a visit.

MELTON MOWBRAY
PORK PIES, STILTON AND HUNTING

Location: Town centre. SK752192

Melton Mowbray is world famous for hunting, pork pies and Stilton cheese. The pies are still made in the town using the traditional, distinctive method of raising the pastry cover by hand and cooking the pie without supports. The best place to go to see this is at Dickinson and Morris's "Ye Olde Pork Pie Shoppe" in Nottingham Street which sells pies baked on the premises and where visitors are welcome to watch the process. The firm was founded in 1851 and is the oldest surviving pork pie bakery in Melton. The shop which dates back over four centuries also sells the "Original Melton Hunt Cake" and locally made Stilton.

Major restoration of the premises took place in 1992, and the shop is popular with both locals and tourists. The mini-guide to Melton provides visitors with a ready-to-follow pork pie and Stilton cheese trail around the town.

Look out also for the swan marking the site of the former Swan Inn opposite the reconstructed Butter Cross. This was the last of the targets of the Marquis of Waterford and other hunting "gentlemen" in the infamous episode of one night in 1837 when they tried to paint everything and anybody in Melton with red paint. This was the origin of the expression "Painting the Town Red".

MELTON MOWBRAY
A PUMP INSIDE A CHURCH

Location:	Inside St. Mary's Church. Ask to be shown the pump by the church stewards. SK752190

St. Mary's at Melton must be one of the few churches to have its own water pump actually inside the main body of the church. This unusual feature stands at the back of the south aisle, but it is not immediately obvious as it is concealed inside a wooden cupboard. The hinged doors pull open to reveal an upright

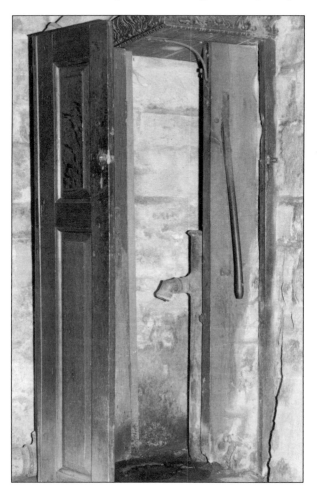

pump still in good working order, the water readily gushing out when the handle is pulled. Although the pump is no longer regularly used, it is thought to have once supplied water for the font. The date of the pump is not known, but the well beneath is thought to be at least as old as the church itself.

Pevsner considered St. Mary's to be the stateliest and most impressive of all the churches in Leicestershire, and it was a serious candidate for the cathedral church of the newly created diocese of Leicester in 1926. It has a wealth of other interesting features, and is also notable as being where Sir Malcolm Sargent began his musical career as organist and choirmaster.

QUENIBOROUGH
THE DOVECOTE THAT MOVED

> *Location:*   East end of the village, near St. Mary's Church.   SK652121

Standing alone in the middle of a field at one end of Queniborough's attractive main street is this impressive early-eighteenth-century dovecote. It used to stand in the grounds of nearby Queniborough Hall, and like similar buildings on estates elsewhere, the hundreds of birds that it once housed, would have provided the hall's occupants with a regular source of fresh meat, especially during winter.

More recently, when the land on which the dovecote stood was sold, arrangements were made between the owners of the hall and the local council to remove and rebuild it on its present, more accessible site. This was done as part of the Community Programme Project. The building was dismantled, moved, and re-erected brick by brick. In total some 17,000 handmade bricks were moved, cleaned and reassembled course by course, by the eight-person team. The task was completed in March 1988 and the site was opened to the public shortly afterwards by the Chairman of Leicestershire County Council.

SEAGRAVE

THE SEAGRAVE SERPENT AND OPHICLEIDE

Location: Inside All Saints Church. SK619176

The Seagrave Serpent is not a snake but a curious old musical instrument to be found inside Seagrave church. It belongs to the time when singing hymns in church was accompanied by a small orchestra rather than the more familiar organ which superseded this practice during the nineteenth century. The serpent required both hands to hold and play it and produced a loud, woody note. The instrument is made predominantly of wood, covered with black leather, and has noticeably few finger holes. Serpents were also used in military bands. They are thought to have been developed from the cornet in the sixteenth century and were produced up until the middle of the nineteenth century. According to a 1930's newspaper article, the Seagrave serpent was in use from 1830–50. More recently it was restored by members of Leicester University's Department of Archaeology.

On display above the serpent is an ophicleide, another instrument belonging to the church orchestra. This was an early type of bugle. It had more keys than a serpent making it easier to play, and was popular in England between 1830 and 1890.

SPROXTON

A COMPLETE SAXON CROSS

Location: St. Bartholomew's Churchyard. SK857249

Sproxton church is some distance from the village it serves, its hillside setting rivalled in Leicestershire only by Breedon (q.v.). Of considerable interest in the churchyard is the only complete remaining Saxon cross in the county. It has a Celtic-style circular wheelhead, and on the shaft below, the remains of intricate carvings. On the downhill west-facing side, two creatures, one a beast, the other possibly an eagle can just be made out. Interlinked rings and leafy vine stems decorate the narrower north and south sides respectively.

The cross has an interesting history. Dating from around the tenth century, it is older than any of the surviving fabric of the church, and may therefore have been an early meeting-place marker or a preaching cross. However, by the eighteenth century, it was in use as a footbridge across a local ditch, a possible explanation for why the cross is now smooth on the fourth side. It was rescued sometime during the nineteenth century and erected in the churchyard during restoration work. In 1951 it was listed as an ancient monument, and shortly afterwards plans were made to move it inside the church. Fortunately these have not materialised and the cross remains readily accessible outside.

SYSTON
MOODY BUSH STONE

Location: Ridgemere Lane, approximately one mile east of Syston, on private land.
SK649110

One of the most unusual standing stones in the county is in a field between Syston and South Croxton. The monolith is approximately four feet high and made of hard metamorphic rock, with five sides at the base tapering to four at the top, and with a slight lean to one side.

Both the stone and the site are of considerable antiquity. An ancient trackway ran close by, and during the Middle Ages, the site is thought to have been where the

Moot or Court for the Goscote Hundred was held. Here the freemen of the hundred would gather in the open air to deal with military strategy, taxes and crime. As such, the stone marks what is probably one of the earliest sites of local government in Leicestershire. The words "MOODY BUSH" visible half-way up the side, were reputedly carved later in the eighteenth century.

Several curious customs associated with the stone have been recorded. One tells how the steward of the neighbouring Mowde Bush Court at Mountsorrel would have to come here and cut a sod of turf to take back there before proceedings could begin. Similarly, other visitors to the Moody Bush Stone would bring a turf with them to place upon it.

WYMONDHAM
A RAGGED TRADE

Location: St. Peter's Churchyard. SK851186

Throughout Leicestershire and Rutland are a number of fascinating gravestones which mention bygone crafts and trades, often with an appropriate rhyming verse. One of the most exceptional of these, is that to Samuel Pears, a rag-and-bone man by trade. When he died he was buried in Wymondham churchyard and given this curious epitaph on his gravestone:

"I IN MY TIME DID GATHER RAGS AND MANY A TIME I FILLED MY BAGS, AL-THO IT WAS A RAGGED TRADE MY RAGS ARE SOLD AND DEBTS ARE PAID. THEREFORE GO ON DONT WASTE YOUR TIME ON BAD BIOGRAPHY AND BITTER RHYME FOR WHAT I AM THIS CUMBROUS CLAY ASSURES AND WHAT I WAS IS NO AFFAIR OF YOURS."

Not only is it rare to find an epitaph to a rag-and-bone man, but also the mysterious message of the last few lines is somewhat unexpected, especially in a churchyard. Apparently, Pears was four times married and had a reputation as being a local character. Strangely enough it was a clergyman, the Rev. Richard Cragg, who wrote the verse and who paid for the stone to be put up.

WYMONDHAM

A RARE SIX-SAILED WINDMILL

Location: Butt Lane. SK850193

Access: Open to the public. Enquire locally for times.

A prominent landmark, Wymondham windmill has the distinction of being one of only a handful of six-sailed mills remaining in the country. Although currently sailless, there are long-term plans to fully restore the sails and machinery back to working order and to grind flour once again .

At the time when Wymondham windmill was built, around 1814, there were over a hundred working windmills in Leicestershire and Rutland. Today there are

none. This is the tower type of mill where just the cap rotated, unlike a post mill where the whole body of the mill could be turned (q.v. Kibworth Harcourt). Its early history is hard to unravel as there were two windmills in Wymondham. By 1910 this one had lost two of its sails, but continued to operate on four sails under wind power until 1922 when, following gale damage, the remaining sails were removed and an external oil-powered engine took over. As such it continued working commercially until 1952, and then for a further eight years for farm grinding. Restoration work started in the late 1970s. Fortunately much of the original machinery has survived and is now on display. All five floors of the mill are open to visitors.

FOXTON
CANAL LOCKS AND INCLINED PLANE

Location: Half a mile south-west of Foxton village.   SP691895

Two methods for raising boats in water existed side by side here at Foxton, one using a staircase of locks, the other a lift system. Both of them are regarded as outstanding feats of engineering.

The locks are still in use and are the oldest of the two, built between 1808–12 as part of the Grand Union Canal route from the Midlands to London. Described as the greatest lock staircase in England, there are ten locks which raise the water level by a total of seventy-five feet. By the end of the nineteenth century, it had become clear that the narrow width and slow speed of the locks was restricting traffic. It was decided that rather than widen the existing locks, a bypass in the form of an inclined plane boat lift would be built instead.

Completed in 1900, the remarkable steam-powered lift worked by having two counterbalanced mobile water tanks or caissons into which the barges were placed for the short 300-foot uphill or downhill trip. Although this cut the journey time through Foxton from an hour and a half to twelve minutes or less, it proved uneconomic to operate and was abandoned in 1911. For many years afterwards the inclined plane lay overgrown and largely unnoticed, but fortunately it is now being restored, and can be explored on one of the many interesting walks in the area. For more information, visit the museum.

GREAT EASTON

THE WELL HEAD

> *Location:* Visible from near St. Andrew's Churchyard. SP848934
>
> *Access:* There is no right of way across the land to it. Permission to visit must be obtained from the landowner. Do not venture inside.

Standing alone at the top of the field is this most unusual stone structure capped by a pinnacle. Seen from a distance, it resembles an outsize spiked army helmet. It is in fact a well-head or well-house, built to protect the water beneath. Locals refer to it as the Roman Well.

Whilst the well itself may date back to Roman times, the peculiar structure over it is more recent. Dating from around 1700, it is constructed from large blocks of

pale local stone. The height to the top of the spike is about twelve feet, upon which there may once have been a cross. On one side is a small doorless opening. Inside, the stonework is unlined, and the well itself has been covered over. Water still flows beneath, although now down the field in a drain. Records show that there were once malt and kiln houses at Rectory Farm, and water from the well may have been used in the brewing of ale there.

Great Easton itself is an attractive ironstone village worth exploring on foot, as is neighbouring Drayton whose church is claimed to be the smallest in the county, and was once used as the village bakehouse.

GUMLEY

A VICTORIAN WEIGHBRIDGE

Location: Top of Main Street at the north end of the village. SP680900

Access: The scales and weighing machinery are on private land.

Situated in one of Leicestershire's popular tourist areas, not far from Foxton Locks (q.v.), this roadside curiosity is easily overlooked. Here on the grass verge is the flat bed of what was formerly a weighbridge platform. Made by H. Pooley and Son of Liverpool and London in early Victorian times, it is thought to have been used to weigh corn from the Gumley Hall estate and coal from the nearby Debdale Canal Wharf. Loads of up to two-and-a-half tons could be weighed. It was last used in the 1920s, after which it fell into disuse for many years.

Its survival and restoration owes thanks to local villagers who took action in the 1980s to save it from disappearing. The bridge and the works beneath were excavated, repaired and cleaned. Timbers were replaced, and when the job was complete, the rescue team celebrated by dressing up in Victorian costume. The scales and weighing machinery which would have worked the bridge are on the other side of the wall, currently awaiting restoration. A similar weighbridge, also by Pooley and complete with weights, stands near the gates of Forge House by the canal in Foxton village.

HALLATON
CROSS, CONDUIT AND CUSTOMS

Location: Village centre. SP787966

No other ancient landmark is quite like this "cross" at Hallaton. A mysterious-looking heavily-built stone cone over ten feet high, with a precariously placed stone ball on the top, it dominates the village green. Well over 300 years old, it serves as a reminder of Hallaton's busier past when the place was a thriving market town and an economic centre for this part of the county. The cross was where farmers' wives came to sell their butter, cheese, milk and cream on market day. However, as nearby Market Harborough grew in importance, so Hallaton declined, with the last markets being held there in the nineteenth century. Today, Hallaton is noted as one of Leicestershire's most attractive villages.

Not far from the cross is a plaque which tells about the village's extraordinary annual custom known as the "Hare pie scramble and bottle kicking". Unique to Hallaton, this much publicised event takes place every Easter Monday. Essentially two customs in one, it is a mixture of pagan and Christian traditions, the origins of which are lost in antiquity. By the time of enclosure in 1770, rents and profits from a piece of land at Hallaton were given to the local rector on condition that he and his successors provided two hare pies, a quantity of ale, and two dozen penny loaves to be scrambled for each year. Today, in a carnival-like atmosphere, the hare pie is paraded from the Fox Inn to the church where it is then distributed at the church gates. Next, the "bottles", three small wooden handleless casks, of which two are filled with beer, are dressed by the rector at the butter cross. These are then paraded from the Fox Inn to the top of Hare Pie Bank where the boisterous bottle kicking competition takes place. Resembling a free-for-all rugby football match and lasting several hours, the villagers of Hallaton slug it out on the hill with their neighbours from Medbourne to gain possession of the bottles in the best of three "games". The last cask is taken to the butter cross where the winning team drain its contents to celebrate their victory.

On the road behind the village green is yet another curiosity — a small solid stone building with pointed spikes on the sides of the roof. At first glance it looks like a lock-up and is indeed often mistaken for one. It is, however, a conduit house, dating from around the late seventeenth century, and was used to provide water to this part of the village. Made of ironstone, it has a stone gabled roof, and inside contains a lead-lined cistern. At one end is a blocked-up outlet, below which is a trough into which the water would have drained, and at the opposite end, a very small doorway.

Hallaton also has a small but interesting museum, a fine church and one of the best castle earthworks in the county.

KIBWORTH HARCOURT
A POST MILL

Location: Langton Road. SP689944

Access: Only by prior arrangement with the owner.

An important building, this is Leicestershire's only surviving post mill. Dating back to at least 1711, it was in use up until around the end of World War I. Then, like many mills elsewhere, it became disused and fell into disrepair. By November 1935 it was scheduled for demolition unless funds could be found to save it. Fortunately an appeal made by the Society for the Protection of Ancient Buildings was successful and the mill was restored. Further major restoration work was carried out in the early 1970s and although the mill does not operate at present, it is now in working order.

The mill is rare in having both its sails and machinery. It has two "common" and two "spring" sails. The large wooden body which carries the sails also contains the machinery which takes up much of the internal space, especially on the top floor. Running down the centre is the massive two-foot-square post around which the whole body revolved so that the sails faced directly into the wind. The body was manually pushed into position by the tailpole, the large beam seen prominently jutting out near the steps. The enclosed base on which the body rests remained fixed. One feature of post mills was their overall portability, and legend has it that this mill was moved here on rollers from another site about half a mile away.

LUBENHAM
CHERRY ANGEL'S HOUSE

> *Location:*   Rushes Lane. SP705872
>
> *Access:*   Privately owned. View from the roadside.

The peculiar appearance of the large building next to Lubenham church is due to its former owner Mr. "Cherry" Angel, a horse-racing enthusiast who celebrated his major wins by adding different parts to the house. The most noticeable addition is the tall tower facing the road which looks more like a folly — it was built to commemorate his horse Alcibade winning the 1865 Grand National. Cherry, so nicknamed because of the colour of his coaches, was a popular local figure. Said to be one of the finest sportsmen and horseowners in the district, he enjoyed many wins, nailing the horseshoes from his champion winners to the stable door opposite the house.

A later occupant, the Rev. Graham Dilley, turned the house into Lubenham Vicarage. A keen huntsman, he lovingly preserved Cherry's winning momentoes, having the stable door with its commemorative horseshoes renovated and hung up like a picture in the house. Today, the door and horseshoes have gone elsewhere and the future of this unusual house is uncertain. The stable block is currently used by a local hosiery firm, whilst the mound under which Alcibade was buried is close by.

MARKET HARBOROUGH
A SCHOOL ON STILTS

Location:	High Street. SP733872

Described as one of Leicestershire's most unusual buildings, this picturesque structure which stands on wooden arches in the town centre is Market Harborough's old grammar school. It was founded in 1614 by Robert Smyth, the son of a local tailor who made his fortune in London. The main timber parts of the building date back to this time. Around the sides are Biblical texts, a condition of Smyth's original bequest. Smyth planned the school so that the pupils learnt their lessons upstairs, whilst the covered space below was to keep "the markett people drye in tyme of foule weather". Above the classroom were apartments for the schoolmaster's use. Major restoration work took place in 1868 when the brick section was added, and the building continued in use as a school until 1892. The building was further restored in 1978. In front of the school is a seat with a plaque to "Gentle Giant" Jack Gardner, a British heavyweight boxing champion from the town.

Market Harborough is an attractive town which retains much of its old-world charm. The Three Swans, a former coaching inn, has one of the most elaborate inn signs in England. The local museum also has much of interest, including a rare vamping horn, formerly used in church services.

STANFORD
A STONE MILEPOST

| Location: | Three quarters of a mile south-west of South Kilworth, junction of the B5414 and an unclassified road. SP595810 |

Situated in the depths of south Leicestershire is this rare stone milepost. On the sides, distances to nearby villages and to towns further afield are still visible. At one time it would also have had a stone ball on the top, carved with the coronet and "B" monogram of the Braye family, owners of nearby Stanford Hall. The pillar is thought to have been one of a group of several which once marked the Stanford Hall estate boundary, but its age is uncertain. Although, it was fashionable for individuals to erect such mileposts on their estates in the seventeenth century, this one must either be more recent or have had further destinations and decoration added later. On one side is the mileage to Rugby Station which was not built until 1838, and it was not until 1839 that the Braye family became entitled to use the coronet and monogram symbol.

Stanford Hall and the surrounding scenic parkland are open to the public. The museum houses a replica of Percy Pilcher's innovative flying machine, his fatal flight commemorated by a monument in a field close by.

THURNBY
REMINDERS OF THURNBY COURT

Location: The Square.   SK647038

Thurnby Court was one of Britain's shortest-lived but most extravagant stately homes, the few remains of which can be seen in the centre of Thurnby village. The building was erected in 1872 at a cost of £250,000 as a luxury mansion for James Alexander Jackson, a Liverpool cotton broker. Designed in an elaborate Renaissance style, it also had its own gasworks and an unusual but unsuccessful underground stable block. Guests were welcomed by the motto over the door "None cometh in too soon, none goeth out too late". The building soon proved too costly to maintain and in 1916, having stood empty for some twenty years, was demolished, blown up with an almighty explosion.

Located in The Square is Thurnby's remarkable village pump. Its large bulbous stone support was part of a well house which once served the residents of Thurnby Court. Water from the pump was used by villagers until the arrival of mains water in the late 1940s, with periodic restoration work since then having ensured its survival as a village feature.

Also in The Square are the remains of the original entrance block to the hall, whilst the ornamental lake which was once part of its splendid grounds is now the attractive centrepiece of a modern housing development. Materials from Thurnby Court were re-used in a number of other local buildings.

WIGSTON MAGNA
FRAMEWORK KNITTERS MUSEUM

Location: 42–44 Bushloe End. SP603987

Access: Enquire locally for opening hours.

This is one of Wigston's surprises — a museum created from Leicestershire's best surviving example of a master hosier's house, shop and workshop. Traditionally, hosiery has long been one of the county's most important industries with its origins in the framework knitting cottage industry. Here at Wigston is an important example of the manually powered phase of the industry. When the last master hosier died here in 1951, the workshop was left untouched and became a time capsule. The buildings are now open as a museum, and a visit is highly recommended.

The workshop contains the individual frames at which the workers sat making gloves, mittens and fancy tops for golf hose. The machines are over 150 years old but were already obsolete even when they were installed here. There were nine stages to knitting a row, but practiced knitters could do two rows per second. The needles stayed still, handles being used to push and pull the top of the machine backward and forward. The frames were last regularly used in the 1920s, although gloves were still made there during World War II.

Across the road in All Saints churchyard is an intriguing gravestone to Richard Brewin, who it claims died in 1718 at the record-breaking age of 152.

APPLEBY MAGNA
A VILLAGE SCHOOL BY SIR CHRISTOPHER WREN

Location: Between Appleby Magna and Appleby Parva. SK313091

There can be few village schools whose pupils learn in such historic surroundings as here at Appleby Magna. This splendid stately building is 300 years old and stands in the midst of fields some way from the village centre. It was founded as a free school by Sir John Moore, a former Lord Mayor of London and wealthy merchant. The original design is by Sir Christopher Wren and it is thought to be the only school that he designed. The plans were largely executed by Sir William Wilson, who introduced major alterations which he claimed had Wren's approval. The result is the H-shaped building seen today, topped by a distinctive central cupola. When the school first opened in 1697, it provided a free education for boys of the locality. Not long afterwards, its doors were thrown open to "all England". Fee-paying boarders were also taken. Subjects taught ranged from the three R's to accountancy, Latin and Greek. Famous names associated with the school include William Huskisson as a pupil, and Dr. Johnson who unsuccessfully applied to be headmaster there. Part of the school became Appleby Grammar in Victorian times but this closed down in 1907, with the elementary section surviving until 1933. In 1957, the building was reopened as the village primary school. Nearby is the site of Appleby Hall where Sir John Moore lived, and in Appleby Magna village there are a number of interesting buildings including the moated manor gatehouse.

BILSTONE
THE GIBBET POST

Location: South of Bilstone, on Gibbet Lane.   SK362045

Leicestershire's only surviving gibbet post stands in an isolated position on the roadside between Bilstone and the A444. It was last used in 1801 when in the dead of night the body of executed criminal John Massey was brought from Leicester across the back of a horse and hung up in chains from this post near the scene of his crime. Massey, better known as "Topsy Turvey" on account of his wrestling abilities, was executed for the murder of his wife. He kicked her into the mill stream at Bilstone in a fit of temper, fatally wounding her.

The grisly spectacle of Massey's body hanging from the post was visible for a number of years. Local entrepreneurs organised macabre trips to the site, and on one such occasion Massey's skull was knocked down and carried off to be used as a punch bowl at an inn in Atherstone. In time both the body and chains disappeared. The gibbet post itself was later found in a ditch and was subsequently restored by Earl Howe of Gopsall Park. It still stands for all to see. Locals are said to give the spot a wide berth on dark nights and claims have been made on more than one occasion that during high winds the sound of rattling chains can be distinctly heard there.

BITTESWELL

A TOPIARY TANK ENGINE

Location: The Bothy. Unclassified road north of Bitteswell leading to the A426. SP539871

Access: Situated on private property but visible from the roadside.

This eye-catching roadside topiary tank engine is a celebrated local landmark in the Lutterworth area. It is the work of steam and canal enthusiast Nicholas Hill, who on moving into the cottage known as the Bothy some twenty years ago, decided to turn the yew hedge at the front of the property into a steam railway engine. The result is this virtually full-sized replica locomotive, complete with chimney, cab, and rear buffers backing onto the road.

The Bothy was once part of the Bitteswell Hall estate. Gate posts on either side of the road here mark the line of the old drive to the Hall from the Leicester Road. The Hall itself was built in the 1840s but was short-lived being demolished in the 1920s. Bitteswell village lies about one mile south. It has an attractive centre and interesting connections with the Twining family of tea fame, one of whom is commemorated in the churchyard by an unusual wooden graveboard memorial.

BOSWORTH BATTLEFIELD
WHERE KING RICHARD III MET HIS DEATH

> *Location:* The memorial stone is in a field near the Shenton Road. SK394005.
> The well is near the Battlefield Visitor Centre. SP403999

The battle which changed the course of English history and brought an end to the Middle Ages took place in 1485 in Leicestershire, in the parish of Sutton Cheney near Market Bosworth. Known as Bosworth Field, it was here that King Richard III fell as England's last monarch to die in battle, thus ending the Wars of the Roses between the feuding Houses of York and Lancaster, and ushering in the Tudor dynasty.

On the eve of the battle, Richard's armies are said to have been assembled on Ambion Hill, halfway between Sutton Cheney and Shenton. Meanwhile Henry Tudor advanced from the Atherstone direction to White Moors, leaving the opposing armies camped overnight little more than a mile apart. Battle commenced the next day, its outcome being well known. The Stanleys treacherously changed sides, losing Richard his advantage of superior troop numbers. Richard is said to have died fighting his way through to Henry, and was cut down below Ambion Hill, near the stream on the land now known as "King Richards Field". The spot is marked by this modern memorial, its inscription as follows:

*"RICHARD, THE LAST
PLANTAGENET KING
OF ENGLAND, WAS
SLAIN HERE 22ND.
AUGUST 1485."*

Bosworth Battlefield is a now major tourist attraction, having been turned into a country park with waymarked trails and footpaths open all the year round. Near Ambion Hill is the Battlefield Visitor Centre, open from Easter to October. One of the interesting features encountered on the trail near Ambion Wood is this hefty pyramidal stone cairn known as King Dick's Well. Erected in 1813 by Dr. Samuel Parr and restored in 1964, it stands over the spring where King Richard is said to have drank during the battle. The Latin inscription translates as follows:

"RICHARD III, KING OF ENGLAND, SLAKED HIS THIRST WITH WATER DRAWN FROM THIS WELL, WHEN ENGAGED IN MOST BITTER AND FURIOUS BATTLE WITH HENRY, EARL OF RICHMOND, AND BEFORE BEING DEPRIVED BOTH OF HIS LIFE AND HIS SCEPTRE ON THE MORNING OF 22 AUGUST A.D. 1485 . . .".

Curiously, a newspaper article in the 1930s drew attention to a cottage in Sheepy Magna whose deeds apparently mention Richard III drinking from a well there during the battle. The Latin wording is apparently similar to that on King Dick's Well. Ordnance Survey maps also mark a "King Dick's Hole" half a mile west of Ratcliffe Culey near Atherstone, whilst there are many other associations with Richard III and the battle in the Bosworth area.

CADEBY

A LIGHT RAILWAY AT THE RECTORY

Location: The Old Rectory. SK425023

There are several unexpected things at Cadeby church — the church tower's weather-vane which is in the shape of a traction engine, whilst inside, the east window depicts a steam train. The explanation is not far away. Situated in the grounds of the Old Rectory next door is the Cadeby Light Railway, the creation of the late Rev. Teddy Boston, Leicestershire's famous "Vicar of Steam", who for many years was the rector of Cadeby.

He started the railway soon after coming to Cadeby, rescuing "Pixie", the engine in the stained glass window and now the pride of the railway, from the ironstone mineral lines near the Leicestershire and Northamptonshire borders. Over the years the collection has grown to include a number of small locomotives; both narrow- and miniature-gauge railway tracks and a huge model railway layout, plus many other transport relics and memorabilia. A friend of the Rev. Wilbert Awdry, the author of the Thomas the Tank Engine books, the Rev. Teddy Boston was to provide the inspiration for the books' "Fat Clergyman" character. His epitaph in Cadeby churchyard refers to him as the "General Manager of the Cadeby Light Railway". Today the Cadeby Light Railway Centre is carried on by his widow Audrey Boston and other enthusiasts, with regular steam open days when visitors can travel along the delightful hundred-yard narrow-gauge track in the rectory gardens.

CLAYBROOKE MAGNA
A WORKING WATERMILL

Location: Half a mile north-east of Claybrooke Magna. SP499891

Access: This is a working mill but it is possible to see it by prior arrangement. Guided tours for party groups. A shop on site open to the public sells the mill's speciality flours.

Whilst many watermills have ceased to work and have been either demolished, converted to other uses, or restored as museums, Claybrooke Mill is an exception. Not only does it still function commercially but it does so using water power alone. The attractive three-storey mill building dates from the eighteenth century although the site itself is thought to be over a thousand years old. Various alterations in the form of extensions and refurbishments took place in the mid-1800s including the relocation of the water wheel from the north to the south end. More recently, traction-engine power was used for a while whenever the water supply was low. However, in the early 1950s the mill ceased working and was left to fall into disrepair. Fortunately the overshot wheel and much of the machinery remained intact. This enabled the present owners to restore the mill and return it to water-powered working in 1987. The wheel turns most days until the water runs out. Water to drive the wheel comes from two tributaries of the River Soar, powering the machinery. The grain is fed down from the top storey, to be ground on the floor below between two traditional millstones made of French burr. The end product is a speciality award-winning wholemeal flour, which makes delicious bread and scones.

FENNY DRAYTON
MONUMENT TO THE FOUNDER OF THE QUAKERS

Location: Corner of George Fox Lane and Old Forge Road. SP350967

This stone obelisk at Fenny Drayton commemorates the birthplace of George Fox, founder of the Society of Friends, better known as the Quakers. Of the actual house where Fox was born in 1624, nothing remains. It stood close by near Dog Yard cottages, but has long since been demolished. Inside the church is the font in which he is said to have been baptised. The font itself is something of an oddity, having been rescued by a former rector from serving as a horse trough, and is mounted on a plinth made from a tree. Fox spent his early life in the village, but at the age of nineteen he left home and subsequently became a missionary, travelling the country, teaching the doctrine of the "inner light". His strong and unorthodox views, eccentric manner and dress, in particular the large hat which he refused

to remove for anyone, frequently led to conflict, persecution and imprisonment. The name Quakers was given to Fox and his followers after Fox told a judge at Derby to quake and tremble at the name of the Lord. Fox gained not only fame and a growing following but also the friendship and protection of Oliver Cromwell. Fox died in 1690 and was buried at Bunhill Fields in London. Nearly two centuries later, a member of the Bracebridge family of nearby Lindley Hall who admired Fox, erected the obelisk in 1872. It has since been visited by Quakers from all over the world.

HIGH CROSS

THE CENTRE OF ROMAN ENGLAND

Location: On the Leicestershire side of the A5, at High Cross. SP473887

Leicestershire's claim to be the centre of England is here at the High Cross. It was at this point that the two principal Roman roads — the Watling Street and the Fosse Way met, making it undeniably the centre, at least of Roman England. Nearby, the remains of a Roman settlement have been found. There have been crosses on this isolated hilltop site for many years. The present one is what remains of a once splendid tall stone monument erected by the Earl of Denbigh and "other gentlemen" in 1712 to celebrate the end of the French Wars. However, less than a century later, damage by lightning reduced its height considerably. The surviving base was moved and re-erected a short distance

away, and is now about fifteen feet high. Remains of the four columns which originally topped this can still be seen, but the square sundial, globe, and cross which crowned the monument have been removed. Much of the Latin inscription on the base is now illegible. Many generations of graffiti writers have added their own comments and at one time an unclimbable fence was erected to protect the cross. It was also where the local youth met for the "athletic exercises of wrestling and singlestick playing". Concern about the monument's fate has regularly been voiced, and it is now a grade II listed structure. Today, there are a number of pleasant walks in the area incorporating the grassy track of the Leicestershire section of the Fosse Way.

HINCKLEY

TIN HAT

> *Location:* The original tin hat is privately owned by the "Hinckley Times".
> A replica is on the top of a flagpole outside the Woolwich Building
> Society at the corner of Castle Street and the Market Place. SP425937

Hinckley is known to many Leicestershire people as "Tin Hat" although few
outside of Hinckley would probably be able to say why, or would know that the
tin hat behind the name still exists.

The story goes back to the turn of the century when it was once common to hold
prize bare-knuckle boxing matches on county borders. This was because the sport
was illegal and if the police of one county came then everyone could flee into the
other county. One such place was near the old Harrow Inn on the Watling Street
on the border between Leicestershire and Warwickshire. According to tradition, a
party of Leicester men were on their way back from a fight here one night and
stopped off at the Crown Inn in Hinckley. One of the company is said to have
noticed an upturned galvanised bucket on top of a water pump opposite the
Crown, upon which he remarked "I see the pumps in Hinckley wear tin hats".
The story stuck and a little while later the publican of the Crown had a large tin
hat made by a local tinker. He used the hat at Leicester horse races where he
kept a drinking booth, sticking it on the top of a thirty-foot-high pole to advertise
his business. So the legend associating Hinckley with the tin hat was born.

When the landlord later moved from the Crown to the Blue Bell, the hat moved with him. After his death, the hat was auctioned in 1911 along with other effects from the pub. The hat fetched by far the highest price of the sale and was bought by Tom Pratt, landlord of Leicester's Three Cranes. Not to be outdone, Tom's brother had a replica tin hat made for his pub, the Rainbow and Dove, also in Leicester. This gave rise to the subsequent confusion over the years as to which was the original tin hat.

The hat believed to be the original next turned up in 1935 in the Jubilee carnival procession at Hinckley. Temperance feelings ran strongly in the town, however, and many considered it undignified to display such a derogatory object associated with drinking. Consequently the hat had to be taken out of the parade. The hat

was returned to Leicester, next making a brief appearance at Hinckley's Regent Club in 1952. Some twenty years later it was purchased by the "Hinckley Times" and brought back to Hinckley where it is now looked after by the newspaper's staff. In terms of size, the hat when filled holds just over thirty-four pints. It is made of tin plate and is currently painted cream and brown. Inside is a holder for placing it on top of a pole.

Visitors to Hinckley town centre will notice a replica "tin hat", albeit of a slightly different shape, on the top of the flagpole outside the Woolwich Building Society. This was the result of a competition for the apprentices of a local builder when the Hinckley and Country Building Society merged into the Town and Country. The tin hat is also now the logo for a local theatre company.

LUTTERWORTH
THE WATCH-DOG

Location: Corner of High Street and Church Street. SP544844

Lutterworth's town centre is well worth exploring on foot. An interesting mix of fine Georgian buildings, old cottages and shops line the central streets. An unusual feature of the building on the corner of High Street and Church Street is this red-brown terracotta dog above the first floor. About two feet high, it sits watching the traffic passing into the narrow road leading up to the church where the famous religious reformer John Wycliffe was once rector. As to why the dog is there, no-one really knows. Speculation suggests that it was most likely a builder's fancy.

A little further up Church Street is a bronze bust to Sir Frank Whittle, one of the great engineers of the twentieth century who pioneered the development of the jet engine, much of his early work taking place in the area.

Both the Town Museum opposite and Lutterworth church are of considerable interest. Along High Street is the town hall designed by Joseph Hansom of Hansom cab fame, whilst lower down is the house where John Parsons-Cook, one of the victims of Palmer the poisoner once lived.

MARKET BOSWORTH
A TOWER AND A STATUE

Location: Market Bosworth Park and surrounding area.   SK410033

Access: The monuments are on private ground with no public access but can be seen from public paths.

Market Bosworth is an attractive ancient market town where for over 300 years the influence of the local Dixie family was strongly felt. The family lived at Bosworth Hall, now renovated and restored as Bosworth Hall Hotel. Market Bosworth Country Park opposite was once part of the hall grounds.

In and around the park are a number of interesting features. One of the most noticeable is this tall odd-looking tower passed on the road approaching the town from the east. Built in an Italianate style, it was once the water tower and centrepiece for the hall's walled garden and conservatory of which little else now remains.

Not far away, on private land just beyond the park but visible from Sutton Lane, is a statue known as the Hercules Monument. Once situated at the centre of a number of paths, it now stands in the midst of a field. The statue depicts the first of Hercules' twelve labours and is thought to have been erected in the eighteenth century, either by the Fourth or Fifth Baronet. According to one source the original was of metal, the current statue having been put up as a replacement by Tollemache Scott, a later owner of the estate. In a field south of Bosworth Park again on private land but visible from the public path are two mysterious-looking stone pillars, both of which commemorate horses.

STONEY STANTON
STONEY COVE

Location: Half a mile south of Stoney Stanton village, off the Sapcote Road. SP493941

Approached by a narrow bumpy track, the view suddenly opens out into a scene more reminiscent of the Lake District than this part of Leicestershire. Steep rocky sides tower above this dark picturesque expanse of water known as Stoney Cove. A former quarry, filled up by water when quarrying ceased, it is now a popular diving centre, with a national reputation as the country's leading underwater centre for training divers. The centre is used for both commercial and sports purposes, with facilities for training, support diving and submersible vehicle trials. Underwater there are stepped floor levels connected by an old roadway. The waters reach a maximum depth of 115 feet, and contain a fascinating variety of "wrecks" including a Wessex Helicopter, a fifty-two-seater coach, an aircraft cockpit, a police car and a boat. Underwater reminders of the Cove's quarrying past include the old winch, rail tracks and the lift bucket. Aquatic life also abounds.

Attractively situated by the edge of the water is the Cove Pub, built on the remains of the old crusher house by Italian prisoners of war. Stoney Cove was one of several quarries in the area, and there are some fine buildings made of the local granite still standing in the village.

TWYCROSS

THE OLDEST STAINED GLASS WINDOW IN ENGLAND

Location: Inside St. James the Greater Church.   SK338049

Twycross village is probably best known for its zoo. Its church however, is exceptional for the famous East Window. This is the oldest stained glass window in England, and contains some of the finest glass in Europe, said by Pevsner to be worth a pilgrimage of many miles to see. On entering the church, its sheer beauty and colours are immediately apparent.

The glass has an unusual history. Almost all of it is medieval French in origin, having come mainly from the churches of Sainte Chapelle and St. Denis in Paris.

It came to England for safe keeping during the French Revolution and was handed down through George III to William IV. The latter, a regular visitor to Earl Howe at Gopsall Hall near Twycross, presented it to Earl Howe, and it was through this connection that the glass came to be installed in Twycross church during restoration work in 1840. During World War II, the glass was again removed for safety, and afterwards re-installed. Twycross church has much else of interest to see. On one side of the altar is the Earl Howe family pew complete with its own fireplace; behind this are the boxes where the family servants would have sat; close by is the Queen Adelaide window, whilst at the west end is a singing gallery.

LEICESTER
TOP HAT TERRACE

Location: London Road, between University Road and De Montfort Street.

The unexpected row of heads on London Road's Victoria Terrace is an intriguing immortalisation of Leicester's best-known detective and master of disguise, Francis "Tanky" Smith. Better known as Top Hat Terrace, the front of the building incorporates sixteen hatted heads. Each one is different, said to represent some of the many disguises which Tanky used during the course of his work. He was one of the first two detectives of the newly established Leicester Police Force in 1836 and as such had a highly successful career aided by his power to mix unrecognised in criminal company. The name "Tanky" came from his custom of tapping or "tanking" unruly people on the head with his stick! The case which brought him most fame surrounded the mysterious disappearance of J.B. Winstanley, the squire of Braunstone Hall. This caused a minor scandal at the time and resulted in a disguised Tanky tracking his quarry half-way across Europe. With the handsome reward he received for solving the case, he diversified into building speculation, and Top Hat Terrace was built for him by his son in 1864. He also developed Francis Street in Stoneygate. On retiring from the force, Tanky became Leicester's first private detective.

LEICESTER
AN ASTRONOMICAL CLOCK

Location: Leicester University, University Road.

On the side of the Rattray Lecture Theatre at Leicester University is this large colourful modern astronomical clock, providing a number of unusual ways to measure time. In the centre is the fixed earth, representing the medieval view of the solar system. The main dial is a deep-blue disk, some six feet in diameter, and is divided into twelve partitions, each with a sign of the zodiac. The white fleur-de-lys pointing to the outer ring of numbers tells the time according to Greenwich Mean Time. The model sun and earth show where in the world it is daylight, whilst the revolving blue disk indicates sidereal time at the triangular pointer by the topmost "12". This singular clock was designed by Allan Mills and Ralph Jefferson and erected in July 1989.

Allan Mills was also responsible for the design of two other unusual timekeepers close by. Above the entrance to the adjacent Bennett Building are two sundials. One indicates "antique time", the earliest time-keeping system in which the length of an hour varied according to the season. The other dial is based on the more modern "equal time" system where the hour is always one twenty-fourth of the whole day. A more detailed explanation is available from the information boards conveniently provided at the site.

LEICESTER
THE HIGH CROSS

> *Location:*   Cheapside.

The monument known today as Leicester's High Cross is all that remains of a once much larger structure consisting of eight such pillars, with an octagonal dome on top and which occupied half the width of High Cross Street. Dating from 1577, the High Cross marked the site of Leicester's old Wednesday market. In the middle of the eighteenth century, increased traffic congestion led to its removal, leaving just one pillar which was re-erected in the centre of the road. The following century, the reforming corporation zealously ordered the complete removal of even this. From then onwards the cross had an adventurous history.

James Rawson, a Leicester hosiery manufacturer, took it to adorn his new buildings known as The Crescent in King Street. Later, it was acquired by the well-known Leicester architect Arthur Wakerley who moved it to his daughter's home in Crown Hills. In 1940, it was returned to the city by Wakerley's family and afterwards re-erected in the gardens of the Newarke Houses Museum in 1954. Its most recent move was to Cheapside in 1976 to mark the Diamond Jubilee of Leicester's Rotary Club.

Granite setts in the shape of a cross set into the road mark its original site in Highcross Street.

LEICESTER
TWO CHURCHES IN ONE

Location: St. Mary De Castro Church.

The church of St. Mary de Castro is unusual in that both historically and in appearance it is two churches in one. Originally a small chapel for the nearby castle, it later expanded to become a collegiate church. To the nave of this was added the huge south aisle, literally as a second church, with its own dedication, separate altar and sedilia, to serve the parish exclusively. At that time, the two churches were divided by a solid wall, and a curious arrangement existed whereby services were conducted simultaneously from each altar. Unusually, the base of the tower is inside the church. The most outstanding of Leicester's medieval churches, St. Mary's contains a number of fascinating features as well as some beautiful Norman stonework.

King Henry VI was knighted at St. Mary's in 1426, whilst Geoffrey Chaucer is thought to have been married here. Outside in the churchyard are some of the best Swithland slate headstones in the county. Opposite is the Castle Green where criminals were once executed. Here at the end of the last century, acrobats would perform on a rope stretched between the church spire and the green. The surrounding Castle Park area is an excellent place to discover more about Leicester's rich heritage.

LEICESTER
A GRAVE INJUSTICE

Location: St. Martin's Cathedral Churchyard.

Concern about the ability of the legal system to provide justice led to this unusual gravestone being put up in St. Martin's churchyard, Leicester. On it is the following verse:

"ENQUIRING MORTAL, WHO E'ER THOU ART, PONDER HERE ON AN INCIDENT, WHICH HIGHLY CONCERNS ALL THE PROGENY OF ADAM. NEAR THIS PLACE LIETH THE BODY OF JOHN FENTON, WHO FELL BY VIOLENCE, MAY 17, 1778, AND REMAINS A SAD EXAMPLE OF THE INCOMPETENCY OF JURIDICIAL INSTITUTIONS TO PUNISH A MURDERER."

It commemorates John Fenton, a Leicester innkeeper. His death was the result of dispute over a game of billiards between his brother James and a French officer named Soules. The Frenchman lost the match and was accused by James of defaulting for not paying the wager they had agreed on. Soules, his honour slighted, challenged James to a duel and threw down the pistols for the contest. James took one but instead of fighting, fled with it to show the Mayor. On the way there, he took refuge at his brother John's inn, but Soules rushed in after him. In the scuffle that followed, one of the pistols went off accidentally killing John Fenton. Soules was found guilty of manslaughter, but later received the King's pardon, a highly unpopular decision as this curious epitaph suggests. The stone has been moved several times, including once at the request of an offended parishioner, and now stands near the south porch.

LEICESTER

JUBILEE PLAQUE, SPA PLACE

Location: Humberstone Road.

One of the more lasting reminders of the ways in which Queen Victoria's golden and diamond jubilees were celebrated are these unusual commemorative plaques which were used on contemporary buildings. The plaques have an interesting local connection having been produced by the firms of Broadbent of Leicester and Stanley of Nuneaton. Spa Place in Leicester where Broadbents have traded from since the turn of the century, has one of the 1897 diamond jubilee plaques embedded in its front wall. Two further 1897 Leicester examples can be seen on terraced houses in Francis Street and St. Saviours Road. The 1887 golden jubilee plaques are fewer in number because they did not sell well, but the unsold stock was redated 1897 for the diamond jubilee and offered for sale more successfully.

The name "Spa Place" is itself intriguing. This is in fact the only remaining visible reminder of Leicester's attempt to become a spa. The terrace was built next the site of a sulphureous chalybeate spring, discovered in 1787. The water was likened to that of Harrogate by the promoters, but its use was short-lived and today the source lies beneath the towering Cardinal Telephone Exchange. At the time, formal gardens, a cricket ground and a bowling green were laid out behind Spa Place, which overlooked open fields beyond. Later, during the nineteenth century the surrounding area was built up and today Spa Place stands in elegant isolation.

LEICESTER
THE HOLE IN THE WALL

Location: West Bridge.

This puzzling "hole in the wall" which greets travellers entering the city from the west, provoked many ideas as to its purpose whilst under construction in 1980. Could it be part of a bridge support or was it perhaps intended to hold a giant pipeline? In fact the truth is more fishy — it was created as a home for part of the attractive frontage from Leicester's old wholesale market on Rutland Street. The attractive twin terracotta panels on either side of the hole feature two mermaids swimming towards the top of the arch with bubbles and fish helping to create an underwater effect. The panels formerly decorated the fish section of the old market. Made at the turn of the century, they are fine examples of the Art Nouveau style. The work of artist William Neatby, they were produced in London at the Royal Doulton factory in Lambeth. When the market building was demolished in 1972, the mermaids were fortunately saved and after a period of cold storage, were relocated on this purpose-built brick structure as part of landscaping work at West Bridge.

Close by is the site of the ancient Bow Bridge, where, as two plaques on the current bridge relate, King Richard III rode out of Leicester to meet his fate on Bosworth Battlefield (q.v.), returning unceremoniously slung over a horse, and was afterwards buried in Leicester.

LEICESTER
HIGH STREET FRIEZES

Location: Coronation Buildings, High Street.

Leicester's High Street was of major importance during Roman and Medieval times. Today, following a period of mixed fortunes, it is again at the centre of the city's retail business, with the recently opened Shires shopping centre along the north side. On the opposite side are some of Leicester's most interesting Victorian and Edwardian buildings.

One of the most remarkable is Coronation Buildings, designed by Arthur Wakerley to mark the Coronation of King Edward VII. It was built between 1902–4 for the Singer Sewing Machine Company and has a distinctly imperialist theme. Across the front, linked by stone chains are six cartouches, a coloured Union Jack

at the centre of each. Animals represent the different parts of the empire: a bear for Canada; a camel for Egypt; a kangaroo for Australia; a tiger for India; an elephant for Burma; and an ostrich for Africa. Above are highly coloured Art Nouveau tiles from the Doulton factory, surmounted by a striking barrel-shaped roof. The Flower Maidens sculpture which once adorned the top of the building was moved after a fire and is now on display at the Ironbridge Tile Museum. Further along and giving a maritime air to High Street is the lighthouse-like tower and the unusual "Sea Breeze" frieze at the corner with Carts Lane.

LEICESTER
THE WHIPPING TOMS

Location: The Newarke, outside the Hawthorn Building.

This monument in the Newarke commemorates an odd and ancient custom. The inscription tells how "ON THIS SPOT STOOD THE WHIPPING TOMS WHO ON SHROVE TUESDAY . . . ARMED THEMSELVES WITH WAGON WHIPS AND FLOGGED ANYONE WHO ENTERED THE PRECINCTS OF THE NEWARKE." This violent-sounding event has obscure origins and is thought to date back to the Middle Ages, possibly connected with the expulsion of the Danes from Leicester in 1002. Later, it became part of an organised attempt by the local residents to clear revellers out of the Newarke after the annual pancake day fair which was held there. This became a
popular entertainment, with the Whipping Toms, as they became known, incorporated into the fair as one of the star attractions. At about one o'clock, a bell-ringer made his way through the crowd to warn of their imminent arrival. Up to six peculiarly dressed men would follow, with handkerchieves over one eye and cart whips in hand. The Whipping Toms were allowed to whip anyone who remained within the precincts of the Newarke. Those who stayed padded up their legs and armed themselves with sticks. Fights often started, no doubt encouraged by the large crowd of spectators. Increasingly the local authorities sought to suppress the custom but it took an Act of Parliament to finally do so in 1846.

LEICESTER

THE STATUE OF LIBERTY AND A CO-OPERATIVE CORNUCOPIA

| *Location:* | West End. Walnut Street and Western Road. |

A number of Leicester's shoe and hosiery factories have been decorated with interesting sculptures and designs. A familiar but unexpected landmark near Leicester City's football ground is Leicester's very own Statue of Liberty. This was the result of a visit to New York by the managers of Lennards shoes in 1920, who on returning commissioned a copy for the front of their factory here on Walnut Street. Shortly afterwards the name of the company was changed to Liberty Shoes. The designer of the local version of the statue was Joseph Herbert Morcom who taught at the Leicester College of Art. The statue has outlived the company, and now has a preservation order on it.

Not far away is this splendid cornucopia, currently picked out in gold and blue, on the front of the Equity Shoes factory in Western Road. Equity itself is unusual in that it is one of the longest-surviving manufacturing co-operatives in the country. It was founded in 1886 by a group of shoe workers who decided to set up their own business, with all the employees being shareholders. Originally called "The Leicester Co-operative Boot and Shoe Manufacturing Society Ltd", the Society's first premises were three rented rooms in Friars Causeway, Leicester. Three years later, a move was made to larger premises in Bede Street. Growing success, especially in the market for quality women's shoes, led in 1895 to the move to this specially built factory here in Western Road. The gateway which the cornucopia decorates was reputedly placed in the middle of the factory in case expectations had been over-hopeful and part of the building had to be sold off later. In fact the reverse happened and the business prospered. The Society changed its name to Equity Shoes Ltd in 1958, "Equity" having been the Society's motto for many years. More recently the company celebrated their centenary and is still going strong today.

ASHWELL
HOLY WELL

Location:	Junction of Langham Road and Oakham Road. SK864136

Prior to the introduction of running water earlier this century, wells and springs were an important feature of everyday life. Of those which survive, Ashwell is one of the most picturesque. It stands beneath trees in a dip at the side of the road, and is readily accessible on foot. The well is covered by an impressive stone surround said to have been given by a former vicar of nearby Greetham. The back is built into the bank of a rocky outcrop, the inside resembles a grotto. A fading inscription on the keystone reads:

"ALL YE WHO HITHER COME TO DRINK REST NOT YOUR THOUGHTS BELOW LOOK AT THAT SACRED SIGN AND THINK WHENCE LIVING WATERS FLOW".

The sacred sign referred to was the cross which once stood above the apex but has since been removed. An iron gate across the entrance has also gone. The well is one of several in Leicestershire and Rutland said to be Holy wells. Elsewhere it has been referred to as a wishing well.

Also of note in Ashwell is St. Mary's church. In the churchyard is the gravestone of the Reverend James William Adams, the first clergyman ever to be awarded the Victoria Cross.

BARROW

VAGRANCY SIGN

Location: East end of village. SK891151
Access: Situated on private property but visible from the roadside.

The small Rutland hamlet of Barrow is an unexpected place to find a sign which warns:

"ALL VAGRANTS WHO ARE FOUND BEGGING IN THIS TOWN WILL BE TAKEN UP & PROSECUTED".

The sign dates from the seventeenth century when vagrancy was strongly discouraged, particularly as it was each parish's financial obligation to support any vagrant who managed to live there for a certain length of time. It was presumably hoped that the threat of prosecution would act as a deterrent, the punishment for vagrancy being a public whipping (q.v. Market Overton and Bottesford).

Today, it is hard to imagine that Barrow was ever a "town" as suggested on this board, and it is tempting to think that the sign must have come from somewhere larger. However, Barrow was once a considerable settlement. The presence of a market cross, the base and stump of which can still be seen, indicates its former importance, and although there is no church here today, this was not always so. The sign was in fact more centrally placed in the village earlier this century, being displayed on a cottage opposite the cross.

BRAUNSTON

A PAGAN FIGURE

| *Location:* | All Saints Churchyard. SK832066 |

Gazing out across Braunston churchyard is this strange figure. Although the subject of much interest and debate, its origins remain uncertain, as does the reason for it being there. Most likely a Celtic fertility goddess, it resembles figures more commonly found in Ireland, which are usually referred to as Sheela Nargigs. The stone itself measures just under four feet tall, by fourteen inches

wide and seven inches deep. The top half of the front is carved with large bulbous eyes, a huge mouth, a collared neck and prominent breasts. Such characteristics were supposed to ward off the devil. At some point in its history, the stone had been turned face down and used by generations as a doorstep into the church, its features seemingly deliberately hidden. It was subsequently discovered during restoration work on the church at the beginning of the twentieth century and erected at the base of the church tower where it now stands, not far from where it was found.

BURLEY
THE OLD FORGE

Location: The Green. SK882106

Burley is dominated by its magnificent hall with its famous Doric colonnade. On the village green less than half a mile away is a building, which although considerably more humble, does have interesting and unusual connections. Formerly the village smithy, it featured in advertisements for Cherry Blossom boot polish in the 1920s. It is also claimed to have been the inspiration for Longfellow's well-known poem "The Village Blacksmith". William Chambers was Burley's last resident blacksmith until his death in 1930, his main task having been to attend to the horses at the Hall. The village pump stood close by until 1952, rumoured to have been moved to the green from the vicarage gates by a former incumbent who objected to the noise from those drawing water there.

From the green there is a short rewarding walk to Burley church. In the churchyard are several exceptional gravestones, quite unlike any to be found elsewhere in the county. Look for the mason's stone carved in high relief with the tools of the trade, and in particular at the unusual carvings on the reverse side of this and several other stones.

CLIPSHAM
THE YEW TREE AVENUE

> *Location:* North-east of the village, on the road to Little Bytham. SK979168

The Yew Tree Avenue at Clipsham is one of the most eye-catching sights in Rutland. Some 150 yew trees, clipped into a bewildering variety of shapes, line the sides of the three-quarter mile long avenue that was once the carriage drive to Clipsham Hall. The work was begun in 1870 as a hobby by Amos Alexander, the head forester on the estate. Family events, items of local interest and royal events were used as the main themes. Amos's work was subsequently carried on by his son Charles and more recently by Forestry Commission staff. The traditional designs which have direct connections with the village and the estate have been maintained, as well the additions of more contemporary themes.

Amongst the many reliefs and sculptures visible today are dogs, aeroplanes, a tank, a church, a windmill and an elephant. There is even a "hunt" consisting of a fox on one tree, with a pack of hounds and huntsman spread over other trees. Clipped in relief near the gatehouse is the inscription "SIR D D-H", after Sir David Davenport-Handley, the owner of the Hall in Amos's day, and on another the initials "AA" for Amos himself.

EXTON

FORT HENRY AND A STYLISH DOVECOTE

> *Location:* Exton Park Estate. SK917114
>
> *Access:* The approach to Fort Henry is by public footpath only. The two mile walk from Exton village through the grounds of the old Great Park is highly recommended. There is no public access to Fort Henry itself but there are excellent views from the public path on the far side of the lake. The dovecote and other buildings mentioned can be visited when the grounds of Exton Hall are open to the public. Exton Hall is private.

In April 1786, Stamford architect William Legg was ordered to Exton Hall by the Earl of Gainsborough to take measurements and produce drawings "for the Gothick building by the pond". The result several years later was one of the most extravagant summer-houses ever built. The history and costs of the building are meticulously chronicled in the Exton Estate Papers with details of work done by stonemasons, joiners, plasterers and glaziers, along with information about the internal decoration. Referred to in the papers as the Pond House, it soon acquired the name Fort Henry, although precisely when or why is not known. Unfortunately the building has since lost its central dome, but nonetheless, it remains an impressive and elegant structure. On the hill above, are the remains of the once-famous Bark Temple.

Fort Henry is one of a number of fascinating follies and buildings in the grounds of the Exton Park Estate. Closer to Exton Hall is this stylish combined bird house and animal shelter which overlooks another of the park's lakes. The tall octagonal structure which rises out of the middle of the building was constructed as a dovecote in the eighteenth century, whilst the semi-circular covered cattle shed below was added later. Inside the arches are twelve stone feeding troughs, still in use today.

Also in the grounds is an unusual game larder with a thatched conical roof supported by Tuscan columns, and between the present hall and Exton church are the ruins of the old hall which burnt down in 1810. It was here that the Mistletoe Bough legend is said to have originated.

Exton church contains a remarkable series of monuments to the Noels and Haringtons, former lords of the manor, whilst there are many attractive buildings and much to see in the village. In recent years, Exton was the location for some of the scenes in the film "Little Lord Fauntleroy".

GLASTON
THE HORSE POND

Location: Down Spring Lane, off the A47. SK898006

At one time, horse ponds, wash dykes and pinfolds were common village features. Today, most have been filled in, built over or have just disappeared. The horse pond at Glaston is an exception. For a while it too was filled in but it has fortunately been restored in recent years. Now in good condition, it makes an attractive feature. The pond itself is rectangular in shape. Three of the sides have low stone retaining walls. The fourth has a gently sloping ramp down which carts and animals would have been manoeuvred.

Horse ponds served several purposes. As well as providing somewhere for animals to drink, they were used for washing horses feet, especially in hot weather to prevent their hooves from hardening. The other main function was for swelling the wooden wheels of carts to stop them shrinking from the iron tyres in dry weather. A notice in front of the pond attributes its date of construction to around 1740.

GREETHAM
HALLIDAY'S WORKSHOP

> *Location:* Corner of Main Street and Great Lane. SK926144
>
> *Access:* Privately owned. View from the roadside.

This strange building was the workshop of Thomas Halliday (1816–84), the best-known member of a noted Rutland family of stonemasons. Halliday worked on the restoration of a number of churches in Rutland and the surrounding area, bringing back pieces of unwanted masonry from where he had been working and inserting them into his workshop wall. The result is that much of the building's original stone, especially in the upper storey, has been removed and replaced by fragments of old church windows, corbelled heads and other carvings.

Halliday was a very successful builder and mason, typically employing over fifty men and boys between 1860 and 1880. He also had farming interests, and on his death he left a small fortune.

Further down Great Lane at the home of Bear, Bear and Bear Ltd, is a novel weather-vane with three bears on it, whilst by the road leading to the church, is a substantial stone well, similar to the one at Ashwell (q.v.).

MARKET OVERTON
STOCKS AND WHIPPING POST

Location: The Green.   SK887163

Preserved on the picturesque village green at Market Overton are the old village stocks with a whipping post attached to one side. These are relics from the time when each parish had its own constable, usually an unpaid and untrained annual appointee, who had the power to restrain offenders and to mete out punishment. In general, use of the stocks continued up until the 1830s when the county police forces were established. Those at Market Overton were last used in 1838. Offences which led to a spell in the stocks or a public whipping included begging, vagrancy (q.v. Barrow), playing sport on Sundays, blasphemy, drunkenness and breach of the peace. A cautionary tale relates that John Wilbourne who built Market Overton's stocks was also one of the first people to be put in them.

Overlooking the stocks from a building opposite is a carved stone head. It portrays Sir Isaac Newton, commemorating his visits to his grandmother who once lived here. Market Overton church provides a further link with the famous scientist, as the sundial on the tower is said to have been presented by him.

OAKHAM
A MODEL SIGNAL BOX

Location: Oakham level-crossing with the A606.   SK857089

Oakham level crossing signal box is notable for being used on the box illustrations for some of the famous Hornby train sets and also as the prototype for the Airfix 00-gauge signalbox model-construction kit.

This attractive wooden building was constructed in 1899 by the Midland Railway Company. It still controls the level-crossing in the centre of Oakham, operating the barriers for what is probably the most frequent passenger train service in its history. The chamfered top panes of each window are characteristic of the

Midland Railway's design, and the maroon enamel name board above the door dates from early British Railways Nationalisation days.

The Midland Railway and its successor the London Midland Scottish Railway erected hundreds of these distinctive structures from pre-fabricated wooden sections made in its workshops at Derby. Many of them have been swept away in the last thirty years, but a few still survive in service in Rutland. Although most will probably disappear in the next few years, the example at Oakham is now a listed building and will hopefully survive.

OAKHAM
A UNIQUE COLLECTION OF HORSESHOES

> *Location:* Oakham Castle (Leicestershire Museums Arts and Records Service). SK862089
>
> *Access:* Enquire locally for opening times.

Here at Oakham Castle is a remarkable collection of horseshoes in an unusual setting, associated with a unique local tradition. Over 200 horseshoes of varied shapes and sizes line the walls of the courtroom in the magnificent Norman castle hall. The custom, which is still carried out today, demands that any peer of the realm on their first journey through Oakham should present a horseshoe to the Lord of the Manor, or pay a fine.

The earliest written reference to this is in 1521, but it is generally agreed that the tradition started at least several centuries before, possibly as a horseshoe toll levied on passing carriages and on the sale of horses. The oldest horseshoe in the collection today is also the largest and was given by King Edward IV around 1470. Many of the shoes were forged by local smiths, others were cast in a foundry. Most bear the names and coronet of the donor. Amongst the horseshoes presented more recently are those from the present royal family including Queen Elizabeth II, Princess Margaret and the Duke of Gloucester.

OAKHAM
BUTTER CROSS

Location: Town centre.   SK861088

Oakham town centre is unusual not only in having a double market place, but also in having two curious covered buildings, one in each part of the market. The larger structure is the town's old butter cross, a heavy-looking polygonal structure which dominates the open area near the entrance to Oakham School. Constructed in the seventeenth century on the site of an old medieval market cross, this once provided a covered area for the sale of dairy produce. It has a tall stout central pillar of stone. Its heavy pyramidal roof is of local Collyweston stone tiles and is supported on eight wooden columns, restored in 1979. On the top is an ancient sundial.

The smaller structure which stands near the entrance to Oakham Castle is more recent. Built on the site of the old shambles, its purpose was to protect the town pump, a substantial feature which can still be seen beneath the arches, housed inside the central wooden post.

The curious five-holed stocks which until recently stood on the cobbles beneath the butter cross are currently undergoing restoration.

RUTLAND WATER
NORMANTON CHURCH

Location: Half a mile north-east of Edith Weston, south shore of Rutland Water.
SK932063

Access: Museum has seasonal opening times.

Normanton church is a well-known Rutland landmark. Surrounded by water on three sides, it owes this peculiar situation to the construction of Rutland Water which, when filled, submerged a large area of land, as well as the lower part of the church. The church had to be deconsecrated, its walls were waterproofed, and an embankment was built for added protection and access. The monuments from here, including that to Sir George Heathcote, one of the founders of the Bank of England, were moved to nearby Edith Weston church. The urban appearance of the architecture is due to it having been modelled on St. John's, Smith Square, London, when rebuilt in 1826. Today Normanton church houses a museum which, when opened in 1985, was Britain's first water museum.

Rutland Water is one of the region's top tourist attractions. It is the largest reservoir in terms of area in Britain, whilst among its more unusual attractions are an innovative drought garden, and the world's largest single-cast bronze, an abstract monolith known as "The Great Tower".

SEATON

SEATON TO HARRINGWORTH VIADUCT

> *Location:* One mile south-east of Seaton on the Harringworth Road. SP913979

Britain's longest brick-built railway viaduct can be found in Rutland, this the smallest of England's counties. Gracefully spanning the full width of the Welland Valley from Seaton in Rutland to Harringworth in Northamptonshire, the viaduct is one of the outstanding engineering feats of the nineteenth century. It stands in the midst of rural countryside on the railway line between Manton and Kettering. The line was built to provide the Midland Railway with an independent link route from Nottingham to London. Work on the viaduct commenced in 1876 and a shanty town known as "Cyprus" sprang up at Seaton for the navvies. A phenomenal fifteen million bricks were made and laid during the viaduct's construction. On completion, a grand banquet was given, a large shed near Seaton station being suitably decorated for the occasion. The viaduct's completed length was three quarters of a mile, with eighty-two arches to a height of sixty feet. The line was opened to goods traffic in November 1878 and to passenger trains a few months later. Today the line is used only for freight, apart from the occasional passenger train diversion, a welcome sight for rail enthusiasts!

STOKE DRY

AN EARLY BELL-RINGER

Location: Inside St. Andrew's Church. SP856968

Stoke Dry church is full of atmosphere, interest and curious features. Supporting the chancel arch are two beautiful slender Norman columns, both almost completely covered with strange beasts, caricatured humans and grotesques — a type of carving rare in England. Near the top of the south column is this cartoon-like figure of a man pulling on a bell rope, thought to be one of the earliest references to bell-ringing in England.

Also inside the church is a narrow stairway leading to a small room which was the Priests Room or parvise. Some sources claim that the Gunpowder Plot was hatched in this room. A notice at the foot of the stairs points out that there is no truth in the rumour that a witch was locked up and starved to death by a former rector in the same room! Another particularly puzzling feature is a wall painting in the Digby Chapel, depicting the martyrdom of St. Edmund. On his right is a bowman, looking remarkably like a North American Indian, although the painting dates to at least 200 years before Columbus.

Not far from St. Andrews is Eyebrook Reservoir, used as the rehearsal ground for R.A.F. 617 Squadron prior to the famous Dam Busters raid in 1943.

91

STRETTON

TWO INNS

Location: The Ram Jam Inn, A1.   SK946159.   The Jackson Stops.   SK949158

The Ram Jam Inn on the Great North Road is one of Rutland's most famous inns. Formerly the Winchilsea Arms, it traditionally acquired its current name through the incident alluded to on its colourful sign. A guest staying there claimed to know how to draw two sorts of ale out of the same barrel. Shortly before departing he took the landlady down to the cellar to show how this could be done. Boring a hole into each end of a barrel, he persuaded the landlady to "ram" one finger in one hole and to "jam" up the other with another whilst he supposedly went to fetch two stoppers. Needless to say he never returned, leaving an unpaid bill and the landlady in an embarrassing position. Alternatively,

the name may have originated from a special drink which was sold there and known as Ram Jam, or it may have merely been a reference to the inn being regularly packed full of travellers. Also of interest is the stone plaque in reception commemorating the famous Cribb-Molyneux boxing match which took place in 1811 a few miles away at the Thistleton Gap.

Stretton's second inn also has a tale behind its name. Although the inn sign features a white horse, the name below is the "Jackson Stops", having been renamed after the firm of estate agents whose board stood outside for a considerable time when the inn was once up for sale.

TEIGH

STRAWBERRY HILL GOTHIC

Location: Inside Holy Trinity Church.   SK864160

Unusual, perhaps unique, is the description in Teigh church guide of its "Strawberry Hill Gothic" pulpit, prayer desk and lectern. Built above and around the only entrance, this peculiar arrangement dominates the west end of the church. The pulpit appears to float in the air, rising about thirteen feet off the ground, whilst on either side at ground level are the high boxed-in wooden reading desks. The inward-facing arrangement of the box pews in the nave below has more in common with a college chapel than a typical Rutland church. The wall behind the pulpit is itself an oddity — painted as an illusory window, complete with leaded lights and background foliage.

At the east end is a plaque recording that Teigh was one of the small number of "Thankful villages" whose inhabitants all returned safely after World War I. Teigh is also noted as the burial place of the great explorer Anthony Jenkinson, the first Englishman to penetrate Central Asia. On a more infamous note, its past rectors include Richard de Folville, a member of the notorious outlawed Folville family (q.v. Ashby Folville).

TICKENCOTE

A MAGNIFICENT NORMAN ARCH

Location:	Inside St. Peter's Church. SK990095

One of Rutland's greatest treasures is this magnificent Norman archway which spans the width of the chancel inside Tickencote church, remarkable not only for its sheer size, but also for the intricacy and richness of the carvings which decorate it. Each of the arch's five orders has a different theme. The outermost one is decorated with unusual v-shaped foliage. Next is a plainer row of chevrons. This is followed by an amazing collection of carved grotesques and beasts, amongst which are royal heads and a fox eating a monk's head. After this, a row of zigzag pattern, and lastly a series of half beast, half bird heads with large pointed beaks. Built around 1130–50, the arch is so heavy that over the centuries it has bowed at either side.

Much of the church was restored in the late eighteenth century. Fortunately the great Norman arch was preserved intact as was the exceptional vaulted Norman roof behind. This has a rare Norman boss at its centre, with two muzzled bears and a monk's head, possibly the earliest of its kind in the country. Close by is an unusual larger-than-lifesize wooden effigy of a knight, whilst at the west end is a former church bell, dating from before the Reformation.

TINWELL
A HORSESHOE-SHAPED DOORWAY

Location: Village centre, south of the A6121.   TF004064

In Leicestershire and Rutland where horses and hunting traditions run strongly, there are many interesting and unusual representations of horseshoes. These include the horseshoes of Oakham Castle (q.v.) and a gravestone in Cottesmore churchyard which features a large carved horseshoe. The horseshoe also forms the civic emblem of Rutland, and inside Brooke church, there are carved wooden cleats incorporating a broken horseshoe to symbolise the passing of the county of Rutland in 1974.

Here at Tinwell, is a huge stone horseshoe, some ten feet high which frames the entrance to what was once the village blacksmith's workshop. Part of the Cecil estate, the forge was built in 1848, and incorporated into the end wing of a pair of attractive stone cottages. Although horses are no longer shod here, this is still a working forge, now specialising in decorative ironwork. The adjoining cottage which was the village bakery up until the 1920s, is now also part of the forge.

WING

THE TURF MAZE

> *Location:*   Edge of Wing village, on the Wing to Glaston Road. SK895027

By the roadside at Wing is this turf maze, one of Rutland's most curious landscape features. It is one of only a handful of similar mazes to have survived in England, and as with many of these, mystery surrounds its date, origins and purpose. Today villagers and visitors alike will be seen walking around its grassy banks but in medieval times the scene may well have been religious penitents crawling on their hands and knees. In fact, its design resembles the pavement labyrinths in French cathedrals, thought to have been used for penance. However, there is also evidence to suggest that Wing maze pre-dates Christian times and as such may have been used in pagan rituals. More recently, in the nineteenth century, it was where according to contemporary accounts "rustics ran at the parish feast", possibly as part of a competition for a kiss from a maiden in the centre.

Wing maze is circular in shape, some forty feet in diameter, with low turf banks cut out to a depth of nine inches. Until 1890 it was surrounded by a bank of earth. Its entire path can easily be followed from start to finish without the need to take a decision on which way to go.

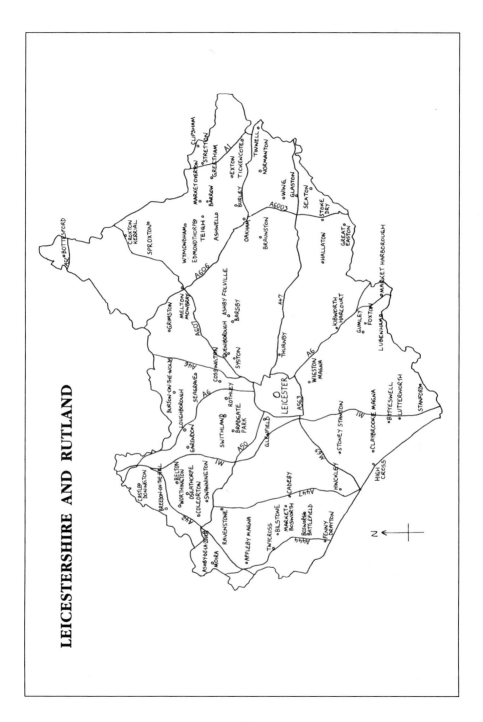

LEICESTERSHIRE AND RUTLAND

BIBLIOGRAPHY

Banner, John, *Out and about in Leicester*

Firth, J.B., *Highways and byways in Leicestershire*

Grigson, Geoffrey, *The Shell country alphabet*

Headley, Gwyn and Meulenkamp, *Follies*

Hoskins, W.G., *A Shell guide: Leicestershire*

Jones, Barbara, *Follies and grottoes*

Lee, Joyce, *Who's buried where in Leicestershire*

Leicestershire and Rutland Heritage

Leicestershire and Rutland Notes and Queries

Leicestershire and Rutland Federation of Townswomen's Institutes, *The Leicestershire and Rutland village book*

National buildings record, Leicester & Leicestershire Committee

Mee, Arthur, *The King's England: Leicestershire and Rutland*

Nichols, John, *The history and antiquities of the County of Leicester*

Palmer, Marilyn and Neaverson, Peter, *Industrial landscapes of the East Midlands*

Palmer, Roy, *The folklore of Leicestershire and Rutland*

Parr, Lynn, *County curiosities of England*

Pevsner, Nikolaus, *The buildings of Leicestershire and Rutland*

Rutland Magazine and County Historical Record

Rutland Record

Secret Britain, Automobile Association

Timpson, John, *Timpson's England*

Timpson, John, *Timpson's other England*

Trubshaw, Bob, *Ancient crosses of Leicestershire and Rutland*

Trubshaw, Bob, *Holy wells and springs of Leicestershire and Rutland*

Trubshaw, Bob, *Standing stones and mark stones of Leicestershire and Rutland*

Vale, Edmund, *Curiosities of town and countryside*

Victoria History of the County of Leicester

Town and village histories, church guides, local history journals, local newspapers and directories

Leicestershire County Council, Department of Planning and Transportation, *Historic buildings register*